Transforming SCHOOLS

CREATING A CULTURE OF CONTINUOUS IMPROVEMENT

ALLISON ZMUDA

ROBERT KUKLIS

EVERETT KLINE

ASSOCIATION FOR SUPERVISION
AND CURRICULUM DEVELOPMENT
ALEXANDRIA, VIRGINIA USA

Association for Supervision and Curriculum Development
1703 N. Beauregard St. • Alexandria, VA 22311-1714 USA
Telephone: 800-933-2723 or 703-578-9600 • Fax: 703-575-5400
Web site: http://www.ascd.org • E-mail: member@ascd.org

Gene R. Carter, *Executive Director;* Nancy Modrak, *Director of Publishing;* Julie Houtz, *Director of Book Editing & Production;* Deborah Siegel, *Project Manager;* Georgia McDonald, *Senior Graphic Designer;* Valerie Sprague, *Desktop Publishing Specialist;* Dina Seamon, *Production Specialist.*

ASCD Member Book, No. FY04-6 (April 2004, PCR). ASCD Member Books mail to Premium (P), Comprehensive(C), and Regular (R) members on this schedule: Jan., PC; Feb., P; Apr., PCR; May, P; July, PC; Aug., P; Sept., PCR; Nov., PC; Dec., P.

Paperback ISBN: 0-87120-845-8 ASCD product #103112 List Price: $26.95 ($21.95 ASCD member price, direct from ASCD only)

e-books ($26.95): netLibrary ISBN 1-4166-0011-6 ebrary 1-4166-0012-4

Library of Congress Cataloging-in-Publication Data
Zmuda, Allison.
  Transforming schools : creating a culture of continuous improvement / Allison Zmuda, Robert Kuklis, Everett Kline.
    p. cm.
    Includes bibliographical references and index.
    ISBN 0-87120-845-8
    1. Teachers—In-service training. 2. School improvement programs. I. Kuklis, Robert. II. Kline, Everett. III. Title.
LB1731.Z62 2003
370'.71'5—dc22

2003028148

10 09 08 07 06 05 04   12 11 10 9 8 7 6 5 4 3 2 1

Transforming SCHOOLS
CREATING A CULTURE OF CONTINUOUS IMPROVEMENT

FOREWORD

I BEGAN TEACHING IN 1971. "BACK IN THE DAY" I DON'T RECALL HEARING conversations about data-driven decision making, continuous improvement, or school transformation. I do remember participating in scheduled in-service days twice a year that covered a variety of topics, typically based on a staff interest survey. I recall that the principal's role on in-service days seemed to focus on ensuring that the coffee was hot and that both glazed and chocolate donuts were available. The principal rarely stayed for the actual workshop.

Much of what passed for school improvement in those days consisted mainly of one-shot staff development events (as in "We *did* Cooperative Learning" last fall) with a focus on "seat time" learning (as in "You'll receive six Continuing Education Hours if you stay until the end and complete the evaluation form"). Moreover, the workshop approaches generally reflected a behaviorist conception of learning whereby discrete teaching skills were imparted through de-contextualized "training." In the best cases, such training incorporated follow-up opportunities for guided practice, coaching/feedback, and reflection upon the impact of the intervention. But such opportunities for long-term professional growth were rare. As a result, many veteran educators find it difficult to suppress the cynicism over "new" improvement initiatives, echoed by such familiar comments as "this year's new thing," "interesting, but there's never any follow-up," "this too shall pass," "one of the administrators went to a conference," "waste of time," and "wish they would just leave us alone so we could work in our classrooms."

A fast-forward to the present reveals a more complex and demanding educational landscape. Ambitious sets of content standards, unrelenting accountability pressures, increased diversity of learners, and expanded societal demands all conspire to raise the ante on the performance of schools while exacerbating the difficulty of making the needed improvements. Indeed, readers seeking a "how to" manual for school improvement (in the conventional sense of "step 1, step 2…") will be disappointed in this book. However, those who appreciate a more subtle and nuanced exploration of school change in all of its messy, contentious, uncomfortable, and complicated facets will find the book's approach refreshing.

Rather than offering a single pathway for transforming a school's culture, the book reveals a set of principles to guide reformation. Stylistically, it resides closer to a novel than a graduate textbook, illuminating its key ideas through a fictionalized chronicle of recognizable educational characters wrestling with the change process. As we follow Joan (the fictional principal), her staff, and the central-office administrators through several intense years, we come to appreciate the book's enduring ideas.

It contends that context not only matters, but forms the crucial backdrop for any serious and enduring educational reform; i.e., de-contextualized reform seeds sown from outside the school are unlikely to take root. It underscores the need to reach a collective consensus on goals— internally embraced rather than externally imposed—combined with a shared ownership for results. It reflects a constructivist conception of school transformation by asserting the importance of changing minds, not just practices, through the messy processes of dialog, debate, and reflection. It affirms the centrality of educational leaders (and not only those with position power) to structure the conversations and stimulate the reflections needed to unsettle the status quo and mobilize change. It highlights the critical nature of systemic support in which policies, structures, and resources are directed toward sustaining a continuous focus on agreed-upon goals and results. And it accentuates the long-term nature of the educational change process, contrasted with this year's "new thing."

The author team is well suited to explore the topic of school transformation. Their collective experience includes many years as teachers, school-based administrators, district-level leaders, and national consultants. Their voices harmonize like an accomplished choral group, integrating the idealism of the visionary, the practicality of the veteran, the analytic perspective of the scholar, and the imagery of the storyteller. The result is a thought-provoking fusion of possibility tempered by reality, promises confronting pitfalls, and a worthy destination challenged by an ambiguous road map. Serious minded educational transformers will appreciate, and benefit from, this journey.

Jay McTighe

➤

ACKNOWLEDGMENTS

WE HAVE BEEN HONORED TO HAVE AN INCREDIBLE GROUP OF CRITICAL FRIENDS who invested much time, thought, and energy into the manuscript: Judy Barbera, Marcella Emberger, Bill Engle, Susan and Wally Epstein, Ed Fuhrman, Tina Lehn, Joseph Serico, Chris Sidoli, Mary Tomaino, and Diane Ullman. Their tremendous insights into the material and into the difficult challenges of leading change greatly enriched the quality of our work.

Two critical friends who deserve special recognition are our friends and mentors Grant Wiggins and Jay McTighe. Grant's thoughtfulness and candor greatly contributed to the conceptual clarity of our desired result: that this work is not a prescription for continuous improvement, but rather a vision of a competent system. Jay epitomizes the professional educator: a lifelong learner who finds joy not only in his own work but also in the work of others. His graciousness has touched all three of us, and we are truly honored that he has written the foreword of this book.

We would not have been able to complete this project without the experience and insight gained from work with our former colleagues in the schools of South Orange and Maplewood, New Jersey, and in Newtown and Sandy Hook, Connecticut. We also want to acknowledge that the process and the conclusions about the linkage between curriculum mapping and Understanding by Design mirrors the work actually done in the Nanuet Public School District, Nanuet, New York.

We would also like to recognize the inspirational educators who individually taught us the powerful lesson of setting the bar of professional excellence high, but never higher than one was willing to face: Delores Bolton, Linda

Darling-Hammond, Arthur Gosling, Carmen Jensen, Christine Kline, Edie MacMullen, Chuck Mann, Jeanetta Miller, Linda Miller, Diane and Zyg Olbrys, Rich Pesce, Jack Quinlan, John Reed, Pamela Silberfein, and Pat Wasley. Through their insights we each have been able to bring increased coherence and purpose to our work as educators.

We would like to thank our editor, and now friend, Scott Willis, who believed in the idea of what we were doing from the beginning and encouraged us every step of the way. His faith in our vision gave us the freedom and the focus we needed to rework the framework and the language until we got it right. We would also like to thank Deborah Siegel and Kathleen Florio for increasing the clarity of our message.

Finally, we would like to say thank you to our partners, Louise Kuklis, David Wald, and Tom Zmuda, whose support in so many ways made the completion of the book possible. Only such caring and understanding people would willingly put up with the long hours and the roller-coaster ride of emotions. They helped us to maintain a balance of work and living and gave us the feedback and guidance we needed to keep writing. We also want to honor our children, Susan and Tim Kuklis and Cuda James Zmuda, who have brought dimensions to our lives that only children can, dimensions that make us realize that who we are and what we do reaches far beyond this work and also gives such work so much more meaning.

INTRODUCTION

A COMPETENT SYSTEM SERVES THE END OF ENHANCED ACHIEVEMENT
for all students. Meaningful growth can come only by focusing on change
from the "inside out": in this book we don't start by imposing on learning;
we start by thinking about learning and moving outward from there.

A competent system requires several significant shifts—from unconnected
thinking to systems thinking, from an environment of isolation to one of
collegiality, from perceived reality to information-driven reality, and from
individual autonomy to collective autonomy and collective accountability.
The school as a competent system has a shared vision that articulates a coherent picture of what the school will look like when its core beliefs are put into
practice. It collects and synthesizes information on student achievement,
identifies the gaps between current and desired performance, explores
research and best practices to identify possible strategies or frameworks to
enhance teacher practice, and then chooses an innovation or a bundled set of
innovations to close the gap between where the school is and where it has to
be to fulfill its vision. It has a staff development program and a related action
plan that are necessary if the school is to achieve its shared vision. The program also must anticipate and take into account the predictable stages of
teacher concerns about the complexities of moving from new learning to systemic consequences. In the process of building a competent system, the staff
members emerge as a professional learning community, embracing collective
accountability as the only way to achieve the shared vision for all students.

Each chapter of the book is grounded in a set of operating principles
designed to provide practical guidance to leaders working to build or to

sustain a competent system. Chapter 1 presents the six steps of continuous improvement needed to move toward a competent system in which everyone performs better as a result of the collective endeavors. Chapter 2 introduces the concept of systems thinking, shows how important trust and collegial conversation are in having educators perceive the school as a complex living system with purpose, and lays out the differences between an incompetent system and a competent one. Chapter 3 focuses on the first two steps of continuous improvement: identifying the core beliefs of a school and developing its shared vision. Chapter 4 addresses step three: the collection, analysis, and use of data to determine the current status of the school in relation to the shared vision and the gaps between what *is* and what is *desired*. Chapter 5 gives attention to step four: the identification of the innovation(s) and staff development content that are needed to close the gaps between current practice and the shared vision. Chapter 6 explains step five: developing and implementing an action plan that addresses teacher concerns and results in successful integration of the innovation. Chapter 7 addresses step six: embracing collective autonomy as the only way to close the gaps between the current reality and the shared vision and embracing collective accountability for closing the gaps. The Afterword concludes with the observation that continuous improvement is an iterative process, impressing upon the reader that this is only the end of the beginning.

We have chosen to illuminate the operating principles through the context of a fictional school that is influenced by our experiences in dozens of schools across the country. We considered centering our story on a district rather than a school but found ourselves coming back to the notion, derived from experience and research, that the school is the place where educational change and all its components actually unfold. We are sensitive to the fact that our school and the conversations that take place in it may appear to be significantly different from your own school, from your own conversations. We have struggled with this fact and reached the conclusion that to create a school that works for everyone would be to create a school that works for no one. We are confident that the dilemmas the characters articulate, the insights they arrive at, and the operating principles they follow apply across the board. The purpose of our narrative and analysis is to illuminate the

answers to the essential questions that frame each chapter, to provoke thinking and conversation, and to invite and encourage readers to apply the questions to and shape them for their own settings. In essence, we want this book
to be about the stories of your schools, both elementary and secondary.

We created a cast of characters with systemic problems to enable our
readers to see glimpses of themselves and their systems in the conversations,
reflections, issues, and ideas that unfold throughout the chapters. In the
opening chapter, we introduce some of the key players in our fictional school
who uncover profound insights about their work and their self-concepts as
professionals:

> Joan, the school principal, discovers that the staff development pro-
  grams she has brought into the building have left the professional culture largely unchanged.
> Susan, Rob, and Maria, teachers in the building, discover that their
  own assumptions about staff development and collaboration undermine the power of their work in the classroom.
> Ed, the assistant superintendent, discovers that his personal excite-
  ment about the interconnectedness of district and building innovations remains undiscovered by staff, who largely see such innovations
  as intrusive on their own work.

The book shifts back and forth from fictional conversation and narrative to
analytic text to illustrate the dynamic nature of change, systems thinking,
continuous improvement, and the building of a competent system. The
unconventional way the book unfolds may be challenging at times but is
essential if the book is to marry theory and reality.

We are committed to the principle that theory and research illuminate
practice, and practice informs research. In striving to follow this principle, we
in effect have challenged the status quo not only in the development of the
content but also in the style of the text. We are fierce advocates of the notion
that all change efforts must be personalized to fit the local context. Linda
Darling-Hammond (1997) verifies that

studies of change efforts have found that the fate of new programs and ideas rests on teachers' and administrators' opportunities to learn, experiment, and adapt ideas to their local context. Without these opportunities, innovations fade away when the money stops or the enforcement pressures end. (p. 214)

Our hope is that the fiction of this place and these people will inspire readers to adapt the operating principles to their own educational settings and compose their own stories of change and success. To facilitate a personalized reading experience, we ask and encourage readers to think about and discuss the questions at the end of each chapter in composing their own stories. The questions embed the principles, support and extend the inquiry from the essential questions that open each chapter, and surface contradictions that have to be addressed within the school as a system for continuous improvement to occur. In raising questions at the end of each chapter, we expect educators in schools and districts to find their own means of addressing them through meaningful conversations and purposeful actions.

We acknowledge the tension between the complex nature of change and the coherence of a framework to think through that complexity (both in the analysis and the narrative pieces). We agonized over the very real contradictions that exist in relation to continuous improvement and the building of a competent system—contradictions that, if not addressed adequately, can severely hinder or stop constructive educational change. But we are convinced from our experiences in schools that these operating principles will help leaders remain steadfast in their efforts to build a competent system. The book attempts to manifest the complexities but also to chart the course for the achievable: competent systems that result in better performance for everyone within the system and enhanced learning and achievement for all students.

MAKING STAFF DEVELOPMENT A WORTHWHILE ENDEAVOR

1

Essential Question

If we know better, why don't we do better?

Operating Principles

– For staff development to be effective, it must be an integral part of a deliberately developed continuous improvement effort.

– In a competent system, all staff members believe that what they have collectively agreed to do is challenging, possible, and worthy of the attempt.

Chapter Overview

The fictional school at the center of discussion in this book is a system full of capable and talented educators who are accustomed to a status quo of isolation and independence. Although it would be unfair to describe teachers in this school as antagonistic, they do feel somewhat disconnected from the system. The teachers are dedicated to the students but are minimally invested in collective staff development. The principal is well intentioned but struggles to combat staff apathy toward collective change.

Transcending the status quo of isolation and moving to a competent system requires a continuous improvement plan composed of six steps essential for purposeful, systemic staff development:

1. Identify and clarify the core beliefs that define the school's culture.
2. Create a shared vision by explicitly defining what these core beliefs will look like in practice.
3. Collect accurate, detailed data, and use analysis of the data to define where the school is now and to determine the gaps between the current reality and the shared vision.
4. Identify the innovation(s) that will most likely close the gaps between the current reality and the shared vision.
5. Develop and implement an action plan that supports teachers through the change process and integrates the innovation within each classroom and throughout the school.
6. Embrace collective autonomy as the only way to close the gaps between the current reality and the shared vision, and embrace collective accountability in establishing responsibility for closing the gap.

The Status Quo of Staff Development

Teacher Conversation #1

The auditorium seat initially resists and then emits a long, piercing screech when Susan pushes it down to sit. "That about sums up how I feel this morning," she mutters to Maria and Rob, who are seated next to her. Before the principal kicks off the year's staff development program, the three teachers still have time for a few moments of conversation. "Prepared to be a continuous improver today, Rob?" Rob flashes a smile back and holds up the morning's newspaper and a large cup of coffee. "How about you, Maria?" Maria rolls her eyes and then displays the "more important matters" at hand, namely her class roster and a brand new grade book. Susan is happy to see Rob and Maria again. She has missed their daily conversations about life, learning, and pet peeves. Susan is a relatively recent transplant; after 18 years in the business world, this is her third year in the classroom. She is respected for her problem-solving abilities and her unbridled enthusiasm for the potential of teachers to positively influence the lives of students. This is only Rob's fifth year in the classroom and he has electrified students with his passion for learning and for life. Maria has been teaching in the building for more than

20 years. She has secured a solid reputation among colleagues and students for helping to move people forward in their thinking and actions in a way that makes them still feel in control.

Susan mentally gears herself up for the first of three staff development days allocated by the administration to make school improvement come alive in classrooms throughout the district. Unlike Maria and Rob, she has brought no extracurricular activities with her to the meeting, partly because she didn't have time to stop by her desk on the way to the auditorium and partly because she hopes that this innovation will have some important connection to the work she does in the classroom. Joan, the school principal, walks to the lectern and welcomes the staff to "what is sure to be an exciting opportunity for you all." Audible groans mingle with the polite applause. Susan sighs and wonders how the optimism and excitement about a new school year can so quickly be overrun by cynicism about continuous improvement. Only 15 minutes into the morning, Susan already feels as if she had never left.

As the lights dim and the presenters begin, Maria notices Joan slip out of the room. "One of the perks of being principal," she mutters to herself as she refocuses on the task at hand (her grade book, not the presentation). Only three hours and eight minutes to go until lunch.

Analysis of Teacher Conversation #1

The behavior characterized in the opening narrative is not only typical but also largely expected on staff development days because of the open hostility of many teachers to any collective innovation engineered in top-down fashion. Although these teachers may not seem to be pillars of professionalism, their reputations with students and staff suggest that they are some of the most dynamic, dedicated educators in the building. How is it possible that teachers who see themselves (and are seen by others) as devoted to their students can feel so alienated from staff development work? Why does "a profession directed toward fostering a love of learning throughout life" seem to be filled with professionals who "appear to have such a difficult time learning from their colleagues" (Wasley, 1991, p. 166)? Visualize the general attitude of the teachers in the auditorium. They are convinced that they will have to endure a day of rhetoric marginally connected to their own teaching instead of doing "the real work" to prepare for students.

If you ask teachers what their job is, they will overwhelmingly emphasize the importance of their work in the classroom: teaching students fundamental knowledge and skills to develop proficiency in a subject area and fostering attitudes necessary to equip them to be productive workers, lifelong learners, and responsible citizens.

> Each hour of every day teachers must juggle the need to create a secure supportive environment for learning with the press for academic achievement, the need to attend to individual students and the demands of the group, and the challenges of pursuing multiple strands of work so that students at varying places in their learning move ahead and none are left behind. (Darling-Hammond, 1997, p. 69)

Many educators have learned from experience that "each time a new wave of 'reform' threatens . . . they can wait for it to pass over so they can get about doing what they 'were hired to do'" (Schlechty, 2001, p. 39). Who in the building would voluntarily attend the session in the auditorium if it were optional? Some of the most dedicated teachers would opt out of the staff development work not because the innovation is "deadly dull" or "totally useless" but because they prioritize the tangible and immediate needs of their individual classrooms over the abstract and fleeting nature of collective work.

Instead of relying upon a staff development committee or a school improvement plan to chart the course for staff development, teachers pilot individual and small-group efforts that target immediate instructional needs in an approach that is highly personalized. "[They] look for ways to grow professionally . . . success to them means increasing effectiveness with students" (Wasley, 1991, p. 18). They generally follow staff development paths that honor individual priorities in a manner that is accessible to and comfortable for them. The three teachers introduced in this chapter exemplify this tendency:

> ➤ Maria is a member of her state science association, attends at least one conference a year on the state or national level, and reads current literature on how to help all students be more engaged and effective in the classroom.

➤ Rob is enrolled in a master's degree program at a local university where he has purposefully sought out courses that will help him enrich his knowledge in specialized areas of his curriculum so that the sources and tasks he brings to the classroom are even more powerful.

➤ Susan works with her colleagues after school on a regular basis to develop real-world tasks they might use to supplement the drill problems found in the textbook.

Although the initiative of each staff member is laudable, this diversity in staff development activities further isolates a school's or district's staff members from one another. Teachers in effect have replaced the collective continuous improvement model with a minimalist structure that endorses the autonomy of teachers to pursue their own best practices in lieu of reaching consensus. Elmore's (2000) research affirms: "Privacy of practice produces isolation; isolation is the enemy of improvement" (p. 20). The end result of this functional, yet fragmented, approach is that staff development becomes synonymous with self-improvement, making it nearly impossible for the system as a whole ever to become competent.

Despite anecdotal evidence that seems to suggest that teachers prefer the autonomy of the classroom, research into school organizations proves that just the opposite is true. Through his research and consulting work with schools and businesses around the globe, Fullan (2001) found that "most people want to be part of their organization; they want to know the organization's purpose; they want to make a difference" (p. 52). Yet, the pervasive individualism that exists in schools prevents the staff from coming together as colleagues with a common sense of purpose and a commitment to improve the system.

Although this individualism may paralyze collegiality at the local level, almost all teachers do feel a powerful global kinship; they work together to improve the quality of children's lives and to prepare them to be lifelong learners and responsible citizens in a future filled with innovation, possibility, and change. The result is that teachers feel as connected to the teacher across the country as they do to the teacher across the hall. What makes this global connectedness a source of inspiration and frustration is that teachers may more readily launch into substantive conversations about curriculum and instruction with teachers outside of their own system because they are not mired in the same local politics and personalities. These conversations may be rich in substance but remain impotent from a change perspective. The freedom that made the conversation happen in the first place springs from the same well of isolation that the conversation disappears into after it is over. Comments like "If only more teachers at my own school were like you" abound, even though the same teacher rarely initiates or participates in similar conversations with colleagues in his or her own system.

The challenge is for leaders to tap into the desire to belong to a collective without jeopardizing individual freedom to do the job the way that each professional deems most appropriate. This challenge, however, traps leaders in an irresolvable and unproductive paradox. It is impossible to lead a collective continuous improvement effort without forcing staff to raise questions about existing core beliefs and habitual practices (to be discussed more in Chapter 2). The key question is, "If we know better why don't we do better?" The answer is that we cannot hold on to our individual autonomy and embrace collective autonomy at the same time (to be discussed more in Chapter 3). Staff members must confront the inescapable truth that their self-improvement model for professional growth will never achieve desired results in improved student achievement throughout the school.

Teacher Conversation #2

Maria, trying to pass the time through the trivial task of neatly copying student names in her class roster, periodically looks up from her task to feign polite interest in the speaker. She leans over to Rob.

Maria: Are you as bored as I am?
Rob: Not sure. I haven't been listening long enough to tell whether the presenters are saying something interesting or not. As soon as Joan introduced the topic, I felt as if I would learn more from the local newspaper than from them.
Maria: You're too new to the profession to have this attitude. At least I've earned mine.

Rob: How many years in the profession does it take to know the difference between a worthwhile experience and a waste of time?

Susan: What's pathetic is that I've been listening this whole time, and I don't think I get where this is going any better than you two. How much do you think the district paid to bring this innovation into the building? I mean, to have you read the newspaper, and you set up your grade book? Next year Joan should just move the line item into curriculum development time over the summer.

As Joan spends the rest of the morning managing her school, two questions fester among the teachers attending the staff development session across the hall:

➤ Why isn't Joan here?

➤ Does Joan know where the school is going during the upcoming year?

After a morning full of PowerPoint slides, ice breakers, and anecdotes, the teachers are released for lunch. The mood in the cafeteria is relatively light as they slip into familiar conversations about their hopes for the upcoming year, ranging from the philosophical (a goal they have for themselves as educators) to the mundane (how many times they have to change rooms). Most teachers eat quickly so that they can steal a few minutes of summer sunshine or some precious time at the photocopier before the lines get too long. Susan, Maria, and Rob are still lingering over chocolate chip cookies when Joan sits down next to them. Her efforts to accomplish a million little things before the opening of school have gone well, except for the fact that by the time she remembered to come down for lunch, all that was left was a bowl of fruit, a plate of cookies, and three of her staff.

Joan: Good to see you! Hope your lunch was more substantial than mine.

Rob: The cafeteria staff make a serious macaroni and cheese. Sorry you missed it.

Joan: How did the morning go? I wanted to join you, but it has been one whirlwind of a day already. I'm fairly convinced now, though, that the buses will pick up all the students, the locker code cards have the right numbers on them, and all teachers will be able to eat lunch at some time later than 10:00 a.m.

Susan: The morning went fine. It's obvious that we're supposed to get on board with this innovation, but I'm not sure any of us are clear on what exactly that means for us.

Joan: I'm not sure I understand what you're saying.

Susan: I agree with most of what the presenters are saying in theory, but they really haven't translated it into practice. How will this change what we are already doing now? How will this look the same—or different—in each of our classrooms?

Maria: Are you serious, Susan? If you think about it, you already do most of this stuff. The only thing new is the vocabulary.

Rob: All I know is that I would rather be working on my own stuff than hearing about someone else's magic prescription to make my classroom a better place. I know what's good for kids, but I need the time to plan ahead so that I can execute it effectively.

Susan: I thought that was what the summer was for.

Rob: What summer?

[They all laugh.]

Joan: Seriously though, don't you see how important what the presenters are talking about is to our own work with students?

Maria: Come on, Joan. Like this one day is going to make that happen?

Joan: It will if the teachers have an open mind!

Maria: Let's take the best-case scenario and say that we were totally open-minded, thrilled even, about the potential of this approach. It still will wind up in the garbage heap with the rest of the innovations that have cycled through this building. What has really changed since I came here 20 years ago other than the clothes our kids wear?

More laughter, then silence. The bell sounds for teachers to return to the auditorium, and Joan promises to finish the conversation with them later.

Analysis of Teacher Conversation #2

Joan has inadvertently sanctioned a climate in which job satisfaction is almost solely defined through one's work in the classroom. Schmoker (1996) explains how despite annual change innovations, teaching and learning practices can remain largely static:

> A school's culture was one where, despite the school's intention to implement reforms or new curriculum, the conservative tendency almost always won out. The culture of isolation and privacy generally ensured that innovations were not really implemented. Despite a school's official adoption of new programs, the reality behind the classroom door was not innovative. Evidence indicated that only the most partial, superficial implementation was occurring as teachers found ways to twist the innovation right back into what they had always done. (p. 22)

This "twisting" by teachers relegates the reform to little more than window dressing as teachers pick up the necessary lingo and fill out the necessary forms to explain how in theory (not practice) their classrooms look different. Experienced educators cannot anticipate the introduction of a new innovation without simultaneously reflecting on the ones that have been abandoned before it as a result of new school improvement plans, a shift in leadership, or the latest buzzwords on the conference circuit. Yero (2002, p. 26) sums up the seeming futility of reform with a pointed question: "Why expend effort on something with the life expectancy of a blade of grass at a lawnmower exhibition?"

Although Joan is aware of the general attitude of her staff toward staff development, she believes that she is an instructional leader in the building, designing meaningful plans to help staff members move their work in the classroom to a higher level. Despite her diligence in keeping up with the latest educational literature and soliciting suggestions from key stakeholders about future directions, Joan fails to create a professional climate that thrives on ongoing evaluation, experimentation, and growth. Although Joan regularly offers to cover classes or find staff development monies to fund peer-group work (classroom visits, interdisciplinary projects, tuning protocols), she has been surprised by the lack of follow-through by her staff. It isn't due to a poor work ethic—some of the teachers work as long a day as she does—but more to lackluster support for building and district staff development innovations. It isn't the relevance of the innovation that has failed Joan. It's the way the change is introduced and implemented that gives it a short lifespan. Joan's basic approach to staff development up to this point has been the following cycle:

1. "Expose" teachers to new ideas.
2. Encourage them to bring those ideas into their classrooms.
3. Solicit anecdotal feedback from them on "how it went" for reporting purposes.
4. Identify another innovation to move the work forward.

Each of these steps has serious shortcomings that undermine Joan's good intentions.

1. "Expose" teachers to new ideas. The result of this approach is that innovations predictably move through the building with minimal effect on the status quo. Lieberman and Miller (1999) explain why this exposure results in minimal progress:

> At its best, it introduces teachers to new ideas and possibilities. At its worst, it makes faulty assumptions about the giving and receiving of knowledge and skills without paying attention to the need for practice, support and feedback. (p. 69)

Too often, an innovation is presented to staff as the answer to a question that (a) was never articulated to teachers and (b) may not be an "essential question" in the minds of the teachers in the first place. For a new idea to move from fad to functional use in a building, all staff must be convinced that if they invest themselves in the innovation, they will be more successful with students.

2. Encourage them to bring those ideas into their classrooms. Administrators and teachers alike put a premium on receiving something tangible that can be used in the classroom. But what does this actually mean? Most educators have binders filled with graphic organizers and development ideas that go right from the auditorium to the filing cabinet, never to be seen again. For an innovation to become actively incorporated into the educator's repertoire, participants must have the opportunity to work through (and think through) how this change will improve the quality of curriculum and instruction; modify the general proposal to the reality of the classroom; gain the knowledge and learn the skill required to use the new concept, resource, or strategy effectively; address misconceptions; and possibly unlearn prior practices. For a new innovation to engender long-term improvement, administrators must cultivate a professional climate in which change is nurtured through necessary allocation of time, resources, and conversation.

3. Solicit anecdotal feedback from them on "how it went" for reporting purposes. Immediately following a staff development opportunity, an administrator will typically approach members of the staff to ask how it went. Although this inquiry may seem uncomplicated, many teachers remain unclear about what is really being asked.

➤ "How did it go?" *Translation:* Did you have a nice time? Did you learn something neat? Did you enjoy yourself?

➤ "How did it go?" *Translation:* Wish I could have been there with you, but I was busy doing some important work.

➤ "How did it go?" *Translation:* I know this was a waste of time, but we all have to do it. Hope it was tolerable.

➤ "How did it go?" *Translation:* Tell me what I want to hear so that I can report back to the board and other administrators that we have met the objectives of our school improvement plan.

For this question to be more than a formality, administrators must establish and support a system in which all educators are required to continuously improve, both individually and collectively. Educators thrive in this type of environment when they believe that their feedback matters, not in some abstract sense, but in the day-to-day realities of their work. This approach means that their responses are solicited both for anecdotal purposes and for revisiting the school improvement effort so that leaders can monitor progress, identify and carry out needed staff support, make adjustments to scope and to time lines, and articulate indicators to measure results (classroom observations, student work, test scores).

4. Identify another innovation to move the work forward. Part of the ineffectiveness of staff development over the years is caused by the mentality that a new year requires new innovations, regardless of the status of the old ones.

Schools have long been criticized for their fragmented approach to change. Too often, critics charge, school improvement has been based on fad rather than a clear vision of the school system's future. This, in turn, has led to one-shot staff development workshops of the "dog-and-pony-show" variety, with little consideration of how the program will continue or how this particular event fits in with earlier efforts. At its worst, this form of staff development asks teachers and administrators to implement poorly understood innovations with little support. Before they are able to master the new technique or skill, the school has moved on to other topics. (Sparks & Hirsh, 1997, p. 24)

The design of Joan's staff development program so far has had more of an alienating effect. Assembling teachers for a mass delivery of information that is unconnected and unfulfilled reinforces the isolationist tendencies of teachers who believe that the system administrators should know better (and do better).

The charge to make teachers participate more actively in staff development and feel connected to the purpose of the school requires nothing short of a fundamental shift in school culture: educators must move from viewing change simply as a predictable cyclical process (innovation to innovation, year to year) to viewing change as a more profound, deliberate opportunity for perpetual growth. In this school, reforms have entered and exited the building with limited results not because the teachers "don't get it" or "don't try" but because they are never really embraced and supported as change agents. System leaders must build stronger alignment between proposed innovations and what teachers already know and believe are important ways to increase their effectiveness and improve their school. They must purposefully bring teachers into the planning and implementation of staff development in a disciplined manner. "If people begin sharing ideas about issues they see as really important, the sharing itself creates a learning culture. I have, of course, inserted an important caveat in that sentence: 'about issues they see as really important'" (Dixon as cited in Fullan, 2001, p. 84). However, this solution is far from a "quick fix"; whether the agenda originates from central office or from a group of staff members, its effectiveness is contingent on whether it will be perceived as an integral part of teaching and learning in the system.

The Path to Continuous Improvement

Continuous improvement, a mantra in the domain of education, simply means an unwavering commitment to progress. What is much more complex, however, is what the particular innovations should be, why they are necessary, and how they can be achieved. When continuous improvement becomes embedded in a system's culture, it functions as "the guiding force that keeps the schools on target in an uncompromising quest for quality at every corner of the campus" (Abbott, 1998, p. 25). Figure 1.1 presents six steps of continuous improvement that are conceptually linear but also recursive by nature. These steps are also aligned with the operating principles that are the foundation of this book.

Although these six steps are compelling because of their clarity and their logical progression, they are not intended to be used as a prescription. Fullan (2001) makes a strong case for the complexity of leading a change effort:

> Remember that a culture of change consists of great rapidity and nonlinearity on the one hand and equally great potential for creative breakthroughs on the other. The paradox is that transformation would not be possible without accompanying messiness. (p. 31)

The intention of this book is *not* to provide an "off-the-shelf solution"; rather it is to prescribe the end result (a competent system). Individual leaders must work in a flexible manner within each step and among steps. This is crucial to the quality and effectiveness of the continuous improvement effort.

A "competent system" is a new concept explored throughout this book to illuminate how systems thinking, collegiality, continuous improvement, and accountability are inextricably linked. The use of the word *competent* as a descriptor is grounded in an earlier work by Zmuda and Tomaino (2001), *The Competent Classroom*. Their book describes the vision and the journey of two teachers to build a "competent classroom": a place where students believe that what they are expected to know and be able to do is challenging, possible, and worthy of the attempt; a place where teachers believe that students have more faith in their own potential when they believe they are capable of meeting teacher expectations. Teachers foster this faith not by lowering

1.1

Six Steps of Continuous Improvement

Step 1: Identify and clarify the core beliefs that define the school's culture.	
Explanation Some faculties may hold achievement in the academic disciplines as primary; others may believe that the social and emotional development of students is primary. Both are core beliefs and drive teacher support for the status quo or the need to change the status quo.	**Operating Principle** • Each school is a complex living system with purpose.
Step 2: Create a shared vision by explicitly defining what these core beliefs will look like in practice.	
Explanation This is the shared vision of what the school community will look like when its core beliefs truly inform practice. It is a narrative description of what is seen and heard in every part of the school community.	**Operating Principles** • A shared vision articulates a coherent picture of what the school will look like when the core beliefs have been put into practice. • The legitimacy of a shared vision is based on how well it represents all perspectives in the school community.
Step 3: Collect accurate, detailed data and use analysis of the data to define where the school is now and to determine the gaps between the current reality and the shared vision.	
Explanation The collection and analysis of data lead to rich conversations among a staff about the meaning of the data and an honest assessment of teaching and learning practices. By identifying the gaps between where a school is now and the shared vision, staff members gain clarity on what they have to do to achieve that vision.	**Operating Principles** • Once staff members commit to the shared vision, they must gain clarity on their responsibility for achieving that vision. • When staff members perceive data to be valid and reliable in collection and analysis, data both confirm what is working well and reveal the gaps between the current reality and the shared vision in a way that inspires collective action.

1.1 *(continued)*
Six Steps of Continuous Improvement

Step 4: Identify the innovation(s) that will most likely close the gaps between the current reality and the shared vision.	
Explanation Staff must have the opportunity to learn what the change is and what impact it will have, both individually and collectively. They must be able to see what it looks like in practice.	**Operating Principles** • All staff must see the content of staff development as a necessary means to achieve the desired end. • It is not the number of innovations addressed in the staff development plan but rather the purposeful linkage among them that makes systemic change possible and manageable.

Step 5: Develop and implement an action plan that supports teachers through the change process and integrates the innovation within each classroom and throughout the school.	
Explanation Staff members must be trained, coached, and supported throughout the staff development process so that they can integrate the change into the classroom and into the system. Resource allocation will need to balance individual staff needs with overall constraints in time and budget. Leaders also will have to be responsive to specific concerns and still ensure that all teachers meet their responsibility for the innovation to succeed.	**Operating Principles** • Staff development must promote collective autonomy by embracing teaching as a distributed quality of the school. • Planning must provide the clear, concrete direction necessary for systematic change while remaining flexible enough to accommodate the "nonrational" life in schools. • Staff development must reflect the predictable stages of teacher concern about the complexities of moving from new learning to systemic consequences.

Step 6: Embrace collective autonomy as the only way to close the gaps between the current reality and the shared vision, and embrace collective accountability in establishing responsibility for closing the gaps.	
Explanation Student achievement holds primacy here, but how it is both defined and measured varies depending upon the core beliefs articulated in Step 1.	**Operating Principle** • A competent system proves itself when everyone within the system performs better as a result of the collective endeavors and accepts accountability for that improvement.

standards but by prioritizing, clarifying, and articulating what students are expected to know and be able to do and which authentic assessments will be used to collect evidence that the goals have been reached, and by understanding how to get students more engaged in producing quality work.

In a competent system teachers and administrators are active participants in the continuous improvement journey because they believe that what is being asked of them is collectively challenging, possible, and worthy of the attempt. Staff not only see the value of the innovation on a theoretical level but make tangible connections between the innovation and student achievement. This realization happens on the classroom level ("Aha! This will improve the performance of my students") and on the systems level ("Aha! I couldn't have done this on my own. I am better off now that the teacher my students had last year and the teacher my students will go to next year are working on the same innovation as I am"). Therefore, a competent system proves itself by allowing everybody within the system to perform better and to be comfortable with their responsibility in doing so.

A competent system is not free from conflict, resistance, or struggle. The messiness in the change process remains, but the tolerance for discomfort and ambiguity increases because people value the purpose behind the change. Staff members trust; they feel safe to communicate their ideas with key stakeholders in the school, to experiment in their classrooms, to give and receive feedback and guidance, and to see themselves on a continuum of sophistication in achieving the desired results.

In an incompetent system administrators or teachers believe that they can function more successfully individually than they can collectively. This condition stems from a fundamental lack of faith among many teachers that they can be "competent" in the system of the school. It is reasonable to assume that lack of a common sense of purpose, pervasive negative attitudes among staff members, and personal experiences when trying to initiate or sustain change all contribute to this lack of faith.

No matter how fragmented the staff may be in a school or a district, the hope for collective action never disappears. Teachers and administrators reflect on and envision how teaching and learning could be improved but may feel their visions are defeated before they are even articulated. An incompetent system, therefore, remains trapped in a series of paradoxes that make the status quo seem insurmountable:

➤ Teachers will pour their hearts into their classroom and into their practice but will bring newspapers and grade books to staff development workshops.

➤ Teachers will swear by an instructional approach or strategy in their own classroom, but the same teachers will balk at the idea that it should be or must be replicated on a systems level.

➤ Teachers will do their best to increase student achievement, but project accountability for the students' failures to factors beyond their own control.

➤ Administrators will emphasize the importance of shared vision but will still draft the school improvement plan with only a handful of staff members.

➤ Administrators will offer to provide staff development resources for individual staff members (money, time, substitute coverage, resources) but will not hold those staff members accountable for documenting change, sharing their experiences with others, or tying their work to the larger vision of the school.

➤ Administrators will release external testing data to the public but will not articulate how the data influence current curriculum and instruction practices.

➤ Parents will support the school through contributions of time and money but largely view their efforts as tangential to key decisions about curriculum and existing and new school policy.

➤ Students will comply with teacher demands, but do not find that what they are asked to do is intrinsically meaningful.

An incompetent system does not imply that the individual members of that system are "incompetent." In fact, many incompetent systems are mistakenly viewed as competent because of tremendous teachers, high performance levels on large-scale assessments, well-liked administrators, active parent associations, and accomplished students. Incompetence resides in the failure of school community members to establish a shared vision, to identify the gaps between that vision and reality using data, and to develop and refine a plan to close those gaps so that the system can become what it aspires to be. This subject will be discussed in subsequent chapters, but in most detail in Chapter 2.

Administrator Conversation #1

At 3:45, when the building has emptied out and the secretaries have gone home, Joan sits in her office and reflects on all the day's events. The one conversation she keeps coming back to is the one with Maria, Rob, and Susan in the cafeteria. Although she initially dismissed what they had said, she knows they are speaking to a real concern. This realization catches her by surprise. These are teachers who are committed to doing what works and growing over time. Why are they so disillusioned by the staff development work over the years (especially Maria, who has been around for quite a while)? Joan takes out a legal pad and starts to list the staff development innovations the school has pursued since she became principal:

- Technology integration
- Rubric development
- Learning styles
- Core assessments
- Cooperative learning
- Preparation for state and national assessments
- Character education
- Tuning protocols
- Extended/flexible time
- Graphic organizers
- Curriculum mapping

Each of these innovations seemed to "fit" the needs of the staff at the time she introduced them, but what was the lasting effect of these innovations on the professional culture? What legacy did this work leave behind?

As Joan completes the list, she hears a knock on her office door. Ed, the assistant superintendent for the district, drops in to check on how the day went.

Ed: So, did the day live up to your expectations?

Joan: I guess the teachers were as open-minded as you can expect them to be, considering all the other things that are on their minds. What I'm struggling with now is whether they really got why I created this plan for them in the first place.

Ed: You mean the point of the day?

Joan: Not sure it's that simple. More like the point of this day, this innovation, but also how this work ties in to other innovations we've undertaken. At times I feel like we just keep walking down the road together without ever communicating where it is that we're going and how we know that we're getting closer. That really affects how you feel about the journey.

Ed: Is it a question of communication only? Or do you see this as a larger leadership issue?

Joan: For me it definitely is both. I want to show you a list of all the staff development innovations I've led during my tenure as principal. What are the common elements? Have I created a cohesive plan over the years, or has my tendency been to target isolated issues for reform?

Ed: Well, let's take a look together . . .

Joan and Ed look at the list and come up with the following common elements:
1. *Priority on student learning needs*
2. *Work to make technology a meaningful and integrated component of learning*
3. *Best practices to improve the quality of teaching and instruction*
4. *Curriculum development*
5. *Assessment of student performance*

Ed: Where have these elements produced tangible results in both teacher practice and student performance? How can you use these elements as a foundation for your next innovation?

Joan: Well, I've been actively working to raise student performance on the state tests by focusing not only on the concepts and skills tested, but also on how to incorporate those concepts and skills into assessments that teachers design for their own students. The motivation behind this effort was to create a more consistent instructional focus among teachers but still safeguard individual control of how they prepare students for the assessment. Because teachers have moved beyond directly teaching to the test, they've become less dismissive about the legitimacy of the state test as a baseline tool to collect data about what their students know and are able to do. This approach, in turn, gives teams the opportunity to discuss the results and to continue to refine the curriculum and instruction.

Ed: That sounds pretty impressive.

Joan: Although I like the theory that we've infused the state assessment into our daily instructional practice, I don't think we've done a good job thinking through the implications or the effectiveness of this approach. If the state assessment is designed to audit student performance for a large population, don't we need to create additional assessment vehicles that require a more rigorous measurement of what our students know and are able to do? To gain an accurate picture of student performance, it's absolutely essential to have multiple sources of evidence. But what other assessment vehicles can we trust—and can we agree upon—besides the state test? Where do teachers need to have consensus on assessment design and implementation, and where are they entitled to do what they think will be most effective for their students? Teachers in my building are very good about swapping ideas and strategies for assessment but remain reluctant to sit down together to discuss collectively the validity of different approaches or the feasibility of using a consistent approach for students on the same team, or the same subject.

Ed: I actually have a different twist on the same problem of fostering a shared vision for student work. You know that since last spring I've been working with a K–12 team of teachers and administrators to draft a mathematics framework that would articulate the "big ideas" that are at the heart of sound mathematics instruction. We first studied the language of the state standards and then compared them with our beliefs about what students should know and be able to do in mathematics. In addition to mapping out key knowledge and skills, we also articulated what character traits we want math students to exhibit in our classrooms—things like curiosity, creativity, flexibility. It's an interesting and totally unexpected dimension of the work that we now want to use as a way to rethink how we teach math in the district.

Joan: Sounds promising! Their colleagues must be thrilled to see the work.

Ed: That's what I thought. But now that they've built this beautiful conceptual framework, they're at a total loss for how to encourage implementation in the classroom. Teachers who were so vocal and articulate in the summer work have now become unnerved by the thought of introducing it to their colleagues. One person on the team suggested that the use of the new framework be given to staff as a model, not a mandate. "Who am I," she said, "to mandate what a mathematics student should look like in someone else's classroom?"

Joan: But wasn't that the whole point of the team in the first place, to delineate common expectations so that all teachers move students forward along the same continuum?

Ed: Absolutely. But now the question in my mind is, how many people must be on board for it to be a collegial effort? There were nine on the committee; I'm feeling as if I need to build more consensus by expanding that number.

Joan: It may make more sense to introduce it to the full staff by making it clear that the district is committed to the idea of a K–12 math framework but also remain open to revisiting the document at the end of the school year. That way they can give their input but are also clear that the rationale behind the document isn't going away. If it never becomes shared, will it ever be worth more than the paper it's written on? *[Ed looks down at the pager on his belt that has begun to buzz. They agree to continue the conversation another time; both are keenly aware of the unfinished business that must be tended to before the opening of school.]*

Although Joan is inspired by her list and subsequent conversation with Ed, she is determined to stop working on such insights in isolation. She must bring staff on board in the creation of a shared vision if her innovation on assessment is to ever get off the ground. Before leaving for the day, Joan drafts a memorandum to Maria, Rob, and Susan, asking them to meet with her to continue the conversation they started in the cafeteria in order to begin to flesh out a common vision for staff development. In the memo, she tells them,

I want to develop a common vision and a plan that will put us all on the same path of continuous improvement for teachers, students, and administrators. No matter where we are as a school now, we can become better learners, teachers, and leaders if we find ways to make our school better.

Joan is both satisfied and dissatisfied with her memo: satisfied because it does give a purpose for the meeting and the work she would like to do with these three teachers and the many others in the school; dissatisfied because the purpose seems so lofty and vague at this point. "It's a starting point," she reassures herself as she heads to the mailroom to deliver her memo.

Analysis of Administrator Conversation #1

Most building and district improvement plans reveal a professional compulsion to move on not because an articulated goal has been met but because it is expected that new goals be identified. Many educators (administrators and teachers alike) have become resigned to this reality, making them appear "change resistant" to internal and external change agents. Schlechty (2001) suggests that the issue is not resistance to change but rather how change is directed:

> Schools are change prone, but change inept . . . In change-inept organizations, each change is treated as an isolated and singular event . . . Even when leaders make serious efforts to move the system forward, they often find they cannot, for the organizations they lead do not have the characteristics required to support and sustain serious [focused] change efforts. (pp. 39, 51)

What then characterizes the management of successful change? Elmore (2000) asserts that "improvement . . .is change with direction, sustained over time, that moves entire systems, raising the average level of quality and performance while at the same time decreasing the variation among units, and engaging people in analysis and understanding of why some actions seem to work and others don't" (p. 13). The first step for sustained and meaningful improvement in any school is an establishment of common direction and a commitment to sustained effort.

Staff Reflections

When Maria, Rob, and Susan receive the memo the next day, they seek each other out to solicit initial reactions and discuss their intentions. They genuinely grapple with the purpose behind their meeting and work with Joan. They recognize her desire to create a better school but remain unconvinced about whether this new effort will improve the quality of their own work in the classroom. All three teachers agree to go to the initial meeting largely to answer the question that is the source of their ambivalence: Is the conversation worth the time?

Maria appreciates what appears to be a real opportunity for collegial work but wonders at what expense. Why is it that when a principal gets a brainstorm, it comes at the expense of teachers' personal time? Shouldn't there be time during the school day for this work? Maria doesn't like to feel negative about her job, but, at the same time, she is tired of empty rhetoric about "collective leadership" when the system always has been a top-down organization. Is Joan reaching out to her by default? By necessity? By accident? Maria believes that she deserves to be part of this conversation because of her experience and insight but remains unconvinced about whether Joan really wants to hear what she has to say. Despite her concerns, Maria decides to attend the meeting because she has been around long enough to know that, for her work in the classroom to move to the next level, it must be connected (and supported) on both the building and district levels.

Rob rarely feels connected to anyone in the building outside of his classroom. He is uncertain about whether "the adults" are worth the time. Rob knows that what keeps him excited about his work is the kids. He views faculty meetings as a general drag on both his time and his pride in his work. From his perspective, collegial conversations predictably degenerate into whining sessions during which colleagues air grievances instead of ideas. This pervasive negativity makes Rob resistant to most committee work, and he is surprised that Joan thought to include him. Rob believes that he has become successful in spite of the system rather than because of it. He has thrived on this mentality, and it has influenced both his self-image and his image with students. Will working with other teachers jeopardize his individuality? Will he be asked to make changes that affect his ability to work with kids? Rob remains convinced that his participation in this discussion with Joan is contingent on the opportunity to address head-on the negativity in the building and what the system needs to do to get teachers doing "real work" together for the good of the kids.

Susan enthusiastically anticipates collaboration with the principal and colleagues because of the chance to think about the school as a system. Although she loves her work in the classroom, she misses the connection to other professionals that she had when she was in the business world. Susan knows through experience that colleagues inspire her work because their perspective, knowledge, and skill help her to rethink her own approach. Susan is concerned that her teaching has stagnated over the past year because of lack of critical feedback and perspective. She feels funny soliciting it from her principal or from her fellow teachers. Who walks around asking to be observed? Susan remains convinced that, in this school, "sharing" has become a dirty word, and she wants to change that.

Summing Up and Looking Ahead

Continuous improvement is reliant not on a fixed concept of success but on a constant striving to be better. The educators introduced so far genuinely struggle with how their individual work is connected to the school as a system and how they can each contribute to improving the system. In the next chapter they will engage in more pointed, and at times more painful, conversations about the assumptions they each have about the job of teachers and administrators, how best to improve student achievement, and the validity of staff development work. What will keep the participants coming back to the table is an emerging realization that they are wrestling with the idea that their competence is directly and indivisibly linked to the competence of the system.

> Essentially, people want to give, especially if it's something they think is needed and worthwhile. That's why it's important to develop ways for people to see clearly how their daily work makes a real contribution to the organization's success. (Senge et al., 1994, p. 514)

Joan's next step: She must now begin to think of results as arising from a coordinated, complex, interactive effort by staff that leads to the implementation of coordinated, interactive structures and processes. She must perceive improvement as a systemic process with a clear common purpose.

Maria, Rob, and Susan's next step: They must move past their isolationist tendencies so that they can achieve a more satisfying relationship with colleagues and perceive how collegial efforts and purposeful, systemic staff development can contribute to their effectiveness with students.

The reader's next step: With your school and your district in mind, consider the following questions:

➤ Given the individual mix of interests and skill among the teachers, can (or even should) a change effort aimed at teaching and learning and addressing the total staff ever be undertaken? Why? Why not?

➤ Will there always be a clash between the school system's interests and the individual teacher's interests? Are we sure?

➤ Where is identity of our professionals rooted—in the generic job class (I am a teacher) or in the school (I am a member of the staff)? Does it matter? To whom? Should it matter?

➤ Have any large-scale instructional innovations worked? Which ones? Why? Why not? How do we know for sure? Is the evidence we have valid and reliable?

➤ Who owns professional improvement? Who should?

➤ What lessons about staff development have our past efforts taught us? Should the lessons be reinforced or do they need to be unlearned? Why?

➤ Are there issues of trust that get in our way? What are they? Where are they? Where is trust strongest? Why? Are there experiences here that we can use to address a lack of trust in other areas? What are these experiences? How can we use them?

Systems Thinking as the Door to Continuous Improvement

Essential Question

What is a competent system?

Operating Principles

– Each school is a complex living system with purpose.

– A competent system is driven by systems thinking.

– Every staff member must be regarded as a trusted colleague in the examination of assumptions and habitual practices.

Chapter Overview

Whether the system is incompetent or competent depends on how it is understood by key stakeholders. If understood through a set of assumptions about current practices and their perceived effectiveness, the system is incompetent. If understood through an examination of the system's elements and their interrelationships, and their documented effectiveness in fulfilling the system's purpose, the system becomes competent. Only in a competent system can administrators and teachers discern what "can be" by bringing to the surface the school's underlying purpose and the stakeholders' deeply held beliefs. Once educators, through collegial conversations, see the school as a complex living system with purpose, they can then understand their work, both individual and collective, as contributing to the continuous improvement of the school, and staff development as an essential means to better fulfill deeply held beliefs.

This chapter focuses on three elements that must be considered if a staff development plan is to succeed in the long run:

- ➤ The school as a system of interlocking and interacting elements
- ➤ The beliefs and behavioral norms that define a culture and their role in promoting or blocking change
- ➤ The need for collegiality

Only through these lenses can staff development needs be identified and correctly focused.

When Schools Are Drowning in Events

Principal Reflection #1

Joan stands in the school lobby in anticipation of the first day back with students. She smiles as she sees a bus pull into the parking lot and soon hears the approaching chatter as students make their way through the front door. The self-doubts and struggles that have been nagging at her for several days are belied by her warm, confident voice as she welcomes students to school.

This is more than a first-day ritual; Joan can be found in the lobby every morning. This habit evolved not from a sense of obligation, but out of a genuine need to see the school in all of its complexity and its wholeness. As she seamlessly transitions from her role as traffic cop to greeter to authority figure to instructional leader, she is inspired by the possibilities that each day (and each year) brings to the school community. Her thoughts for the moment settle on this last role: instructional leader. She surveys the diversity of the student body, perceiving ranges in background, abilities, interests, and styles. She thinks of the teachers these students will work with and considers the various ways the teachers reach different students and convey subject matter. It fascinates her to think about how relationships between student and teacher begin because of a computer program designed to create a functional schedule. Out of this initially sterile context, powerful relationships emerge as student and teacher study each other's strengths and weaknesses, likes and dislikes, expectations and limits, and try to use their understanding to their advantage. While deep in thought, Joan notices that the mission statement hanging next to the main entrance is slightly crooked. As she straightens it, she reads the words she already knows by heart: "To challenge our students to pursue excellence and a love of learning in a state-of-the-art facility." Encouraging a pursuit of excellence and a love of learning is a worthy endeavor but a difficult one to achieve for all students because of the need to balance sometimes divergent concerns. Joan wonders, at what point does the emphasis on standards and state assessments block passion in the classroom for both student and teacher? How do I convince teachers that they don't really have to "teach to the test"? How can I increase their confidence in locally designed assessments? How do I convince students that they can achieve their goals, whether set by state mandates, teacher directives, or personal ambitions?

Joan's weighty internal conversation abruptly stops when the second bell rings, signaling the start of the first class. As the lobby once again becomes quiet, Joan sighs and bends down to pick up several wrappers discarded on the freshly shampooed carpet. Maria, who happens to walk by right at that moment, flashes a smile acknowledging Joan's additional role as head custodian. "Great to be back, huh?" says Maria. "More than you know," Joan sincerely replies.

Once Joan returns to the main office, she is immediately faced with a typical tidal wave of unforeseen problems that arise from her multiple roles. A school bus is delayed because of a traffic jam; a student is hurt and needs Joan's attention; a teacher has to leave because her child is ill and there is no coverage for her class; a parent has called to say that her child is afraid of math, and another is asking that his child's teacher be required to read some articles he has researched so that his son's learning needs will be better understood; a teacher demands that a student he had last year be dropped from his roster this year.

Analysis of Principal Reflection #1

The deluge of problems that Joan encounters within five minutes of opening the school demands her immediate attention; this leads to a common malady that plagues many administrators: a school "drowning in events" (Senge et al., 2000, p. 77). Joan diligently works her way through problems one by one but rarely takes the time to understand how these events and elements relate—or even to consider the possibility that they do relate. This approach to running a school traps administrators in the everyday routine of schooling in which pressing problems sap their energy, spirit, and attention. As Joan gets wrapped up in the "happenings" at her school, she loses her earlier insights about how her decisions affect the operations that define the system as a whole.

While Joan's preoccupation with these events seems to be a normal response (even a desirable response for the manager of the school), her determination to "resolve problems" blocks her ability to appreciate the interrelationships of problems and solutions within the context of the organization. Joan struggles to "find the time" to think about the "big-picture issues" of the school. Each problem seems more urgent than the ambiguous inquiry into the school as a system. In *The Seven Habits of Highly Effective People*, Stephen Covey (1989) vividly describes what it feels like when a person functions almost exclusively as a crisis manager:

> It keeps getting bigger and bigger until it dominates you. It's like the pounding surf. A huge problem comes and knocks you down and you're wiped out. You struggle back up only to face another one that knocks you down and slams you to the ground. (p. 152)

It is understandable that administrators treat a problem as something to be conquered, endured, avoided, or ignored. However, this antagonistic approach drains energy and good will while leaving the status quo largely intact. To conquer a problem is to destroy only the immediate symptoms. To endure the problem is to attempt to outlast it. To avoid a problem is to dodge it over and over again. To ignore the problem is to pretend it does not exist. But no matter what strategy is used, it will only leave the problem and its underlying causes unresolved. Staff members are left with a collection of elements whose perceived interrelationship is tenuous at best, seemingly random at worst. Problems continue to emerge without any systemic approach to solve them.

Staff Conversation #1

Joan begins to hammer away at the list of pressing problems. She calls four teachers in their classrooms before she finally can arrange enough coverage for the students of the teacher who must return home to a sick child. She writes a general announcement to be copied and delivered to each classroom alerting teachers to the delayed bus and the students who will be coming to classes late. Before she can get the announcement to the secretary to duplicate, a call is put through from the parent whose child is afraid of math. The parent makes it clear that she had hoped to hear from Joan earlier. Joan apologizes but is somewhat angry. She asks herself, "Why can't people understand that their problem is not my only problem?" Joan tries to listen patiently to the parent but remains preoccupied with getting the notice to the teachers before the bus arrives. Although she does not want to appear insensitive, Joan interrupts the parent's monologue to say she will speak to the girl before she goes into math. The mother asks that Joan call back and let her know how the conversation went. Now one problem has spawned several jobs: tracking down the student, addressing the concern, contacting the parent. None of these jobs is difficult or overwhelming, but the totality of small jobs makes Joan feel frustrated. As she finishes jotting a note to herself to remember to follow up with the parent, the secretary steps in to say that Ed is on the phone. Joan picks up the phone, places her hand over the mouthpiece, and tells the secretary to duplicate the announcement and make sure it is delivered immediately.

Secretary: How am I supposed to get it to all the teachers?

Joan: I don't care, just get it to them. [*Taking a deep breath*] Sorry, Ed. What's up?

Ed: Just called with a question from a board member about lockers.

Joan: Fantastic. Another thing that needed to be taken care of five minutes ago, I'm sure.

Ed: What's up?

Joan: It's the first day of school and I'm drowning in problems. Now a board member wants to know about lockers! I don't have time right now, Ed. OK?

Ed: Right. This can wait until the end of the day. Are the problems serious?

Joan: What problem isn't, at least in the eyes of the person wanting it addressed?

Ed: I'll be in your neck of the woods late this afternoon. I'll drop by then and discuss the locker issue. It can wait until you get your building under control.

As she hangs up the phone, Joan immediately regrets that she has given Ed the impression that she is having a tough time. Although that impression may not be far off the mark, Joan believes administrators have an unwritten rule that those kinds of feelings can be expressed only to educators whom you are likely never to see again. "When am I going to learn to keep my mouth shut?" Her self-reprimand is cut short as she suddenly remembers the child who was injured earlier. She jumps up and runs out to the front of the main office to find it unattended: no child, no secretary. Obviously the secretary is out delivering the announcement. Joan picks up the phone and calls the nurse.

Nurse: Oh, yes, the child is here, waiting for you.

Joan: Is she OK?

Nurse: Well, she has quite a scrape, but I suspect she'll live. She's just shaken. It might be nice for you to talk with her before she goes back to class.

Now Joan has two more problems—covering the office until the secretary returns and then getting over to the nurse's office to talk to the student with the scrape. Joan is taking a phone message for a teacher about his mortgage when the secretary returns from running around to each classroom to deliver the announcement about the late bus. They flash each other an annoyed glance, the secretary expressing her feelings about being sent on a mad dash around the building and Joan expressing hers for having to answer phones when she has so many other things to do. And so Joan's day goes.

After seeing the buses off at the end of the day, Joan is back at her desk sorting through the tasks that still have to be dealt with before she can go home. Ed walks in; Joan is momentarily surprised. She completely forgot that he said he would drop by.

➤

Joan: Oh! Hi, Ed. Let me see, you're here about a locker problem, right?

Ed: Overwhelmed?

Joan: No, why do you ask?

Ed: You seemed a little overwhelmed when we talked this morning, and then your comment about the pile of issues that have already cluttered your desk, and it's only the first day.

Joan: I didn't say that.

Ed: Joan, don't get defensive. I promise I'm here to help. I know how skilled you are as a manager so I know there has to be good grounds for your feelings of pressure. Tell me about your day; tell me about the problems.

Joan: Oh, it's nothing. New year, same problems—demanding parents; a child who is math phobic; a child with special learning needs; a kid who is shaken up by a fall; a teacher who wants a kid out of his class; a late bus; a teacher with a sick kid at home who has to have care. Nothing that I can't handle.

Ed: I'm a little puzzled. Why are all these your jobs? Next you'll be telling me you'll be calling home tomorrow when a kid doesn't bring in her homework.

Joan: Actually, once in a while I do that, but only when a teacher asks me to. It's important to me that when people need me, I'm there for them. That's how I see myself as a principal: to help make quality learning possible.

Ed: Joan, I'm going to be frank: you can't do everything. There's a pattern here. You may see yourself collaborating with everyone, but in a real sense you aren't. You've been solving problems *for* them, not *with* them in the interests of the school. You have to give some of it away to staff members who can handle it as well as you can—or even better, given the current pressures to make so many decisions.

Joan: What do you mean? Give me a for instance.

As the conversation unfolds, Ed suggests that the nurse could have treated the wound and the girl's psyche; the guidance counselor could have dealt with the math phobia and the child with the special learning needs; the secretary could have written the announcement about the late bus and sent it out in a manner pre-prescribed for such situations but not one that leaves the office unattended. In fact, the secretary also could have provided the coverage for the teacher with the sick child which would have conformed with the district regulation that clearly spells out how to assign emergency coverage. Joan needed to manage patterns of problems, not deal with each individual problem. Joan heard Ed and found his position made sense.

Joan: But we've never done things that way, Ed.

Ed: Don't assume the way you've always done it is the best way. I think you should think of the pattern here. Something has got to change if you're going to be able to be the instructional leader that I know you always say is the real source of satisfaction for you.

Joan: *[With a grin]* And what about the locker problem?

Ed: The board member wanted you to serve on a committee to decide what lockers we should buy for the new middle school. I'll just tell him that although you would love to work with him, you really want to focus on instruction this year, right?

Analysis of Staff Conversation #1

Although Joan can't stand in the hallway all day and follow her train of thought, she can change how she works throughout her day. The priority for Joan becomes finding a way to sustain the systems thinking mind-set she experiences in the lobby. Making that happen requires something other than self-discipline; it requires "putting first things first" (Covey, 1989, p. 148). To think systemically, Joan needs to recognize and resolve the disconnectedness between the "business of running a school" that consumes her in the main office and her desire to be more involved with the "real work" that happens in the classroom.

As clichéd as it might sound, perspective matters. As Fullan (1999) observes,

> Problems are necessary for learning, but not without a capacity for inquiry to learn the right lessons. It seems perverse to say that problems are our friends, but we cannot develop effective responses to complex situations unless we actively seek and confront the real problems which are in fact difficult to solve. (p. 26)

When administrators and staff see their school in terms of this chapter's first operating principle—*Each school is a complex living system with purpose*—they reclaim the ability to evaluate the effectiveness of the system and their role in bringing about necessary change. The operating principle is brief but expresses a complicated concept. The words have been carefully chosen to reflect the thinking process that lives in the minds of administrators and staff in a competent system.

A Complex Living System. To see the school as a complex, living system, educators must spend time thinking through both the obvious and the more subtle interrelationships among the various elements of the school. To play out this idea, consider the selection of a new textbook. The new textbook must meet staff expectations and state standards for what students should know and be able to do. No matter how closely the book is aligned with these expectations, however, adopting it will require some curriculum revision to eliminate gaps and repetitions as well as to integrate new ideas and assessments. But change a part of the curriculum and you must consider the likely systemic consequences. What if the rich assessment ideas that attracted teachers to the text in the first place are impossible to execute without increased instructional time? And what if without that extra time the assessment ideas become irrelevant, prompting some teachers to demand a return to the former textbook? Change happens within a complex system of interrelated elements. Educators must contemplate the elements, interrelate the various elements, discern the patterns that constitute the whole, and think through how to redesign, over time, the patterns for learning and growth to ensure that the school's purpose is achieved. When Joan goes out into the lobby on the first day of school, the system becomes alive for her. When she goes back into her office, the systems thinking recedes into the background as she resumes the job of managing the school. All of the patterns that make up the living system are always present, but unless people perceive the connections and analyze a situation in that context, they are blind to reality. Almost every educator has experienced the uproar that can result from a failure to anticipate the ripple effect of a single innovation.

Another layer of complexity in any system is triggered by the annual change in the student body, the parents, and the staff. Assume, for the moment, that the systemic changes have been considered and adequately addressed—all of the staff is on board, all of the students comprehend the new system, and the parents support it. And then over time, the staff, student body, and parents change. The challenge here is to ensure that new stakeholders are supported as they acclimate to the school's culture. Although this annual turnover is predictable, the specific needs that result are not. School goals will need to be reexamined to verify whether the allocation of resources is still appropriate and whether new priorities have emerged.

A Purposeful System. To see the school as a purposeful system, educators must articulate and affirm the deeply held, defining beliefs that give purpose to their work. There must be a wholeness whose interacting elements "continually affect each other over time and operate toward a common purpose" (Senge et. al, 1994, p. 90). Staff members may define their purpose in various ways:

➤ A staff can believe that their purpose is to serve the needs of all students.
➤ A staff can believe that they must first serve the subject they teach.
➤ A staff can believe that their chief purpose is to provide a safe and secure environment.

Without clear, explicit definition and mutual agreement on the "purpose" of school, it becomes difficult to meet each other's needs, to assess one's own adequacy, or to measure progress meaningfully. Senge et. al (2000) has commented on how various stakeholders can offer differing perspectives on this matter:

> All people know what they want from education. The parent wants the child to be successful—or perhaps, simply to learn to read. The teacher wants to create a terrific curriculum, encompassing not just intellectual skills but athletics, music, art, and socially adept behavior—or, perhaps, to have a high-performing class. . . . And the child wants to learn what the child wants to learn—whether it's to read right now, to dive off the high board, to build things, to play music, to make friends, or simply to be him or herself. (p. 72)

For a school to be more than a loose confederation of independent learning environments, all stakeholders must be clear on the beliefs that give collective and concrete purpose to their individual efforts. Otherwise, a success or a failure can be dismissed as an isolated case in which this teacher working with this student in this environment produced a result that is interesting but holds minimal value as a trend or a pattern because the variables for teaching and learning change so much from year to year (and room to room).

Principal Reflection #2

As the first week of school ends, Joan sinks into her chair and absent-mindedly shuffles through the messages neatly stacked on her blotter. She clicks on the radio so that the jazz music can soothe her throbbing head as well as make the building feel less empty. It is amazing how the whole place sounds and feels different on a late Friday afternoon. Joan scans her calendar for the upcoming week. Slated for Wednesday afternoon is the meeting with Maria, Rob, and Susan. Joan instantly remembers the conversation in the cafeteria but feels far removed from the sense of urgency that prompted this upcoming meeting. When she first became a principal more than eight years ago, this would have been exactly the kind of conversation she would have looked forward to having with a group of teachers. That was before she realized how much time it took to get a janitor to fix a broken urinal, to make sure that bus #12 no longer delivered students to school five minutes late, and to iron out the glitches in the school scheduling software. Joan forces her brain to kick into gear and recreates the line of inquiry that got her thinking about the purpose of the school. After several minutes of brainstorming, she arrives at the following four conclusions:

1. I play a key role in making the school what it is.
2. My role is dramatically enhanced when I feel a strong connection with my staff.
3. Every staff member plays a key role in making the school what it is.
4. All staff members can be more successful if they work together.

The conclusions seem both breathtaking and boring. Is it worth pulling the teachers away from other "things" they could be doing to discuss these ideas? On a cognitive level, she knows that for a school to operate with a common sense of purpose, there must be collaboration in uncovering that purpose. On an emotional level, she knows that she doesn't have the confidence or the clarity she is accustomed to having in her work with staff, and this makes her seriously consider abandoning the conversation "for now" until she can spend more time privately working through the issues. She finally decides, more out of a sense of obligation than anything else, to keep the meeting with the three teachers and see what happens.

Analysis of Principal Reflection #2

Joan now faces the challenge suggested by the second operating principle of this chapter: *A competent system is driven by systems thinking.* She must pave the way for systems thinking not only for herself but also for her staff members, who are likely to be even further removed from thinking about the school in its wholeness and complexity. Lieberman and Miller (1999) suggest that many teachers will need to learn how to think systemically. "This kind of thinking is not intuitive—especially for people who have been thinking in terms of my classroom and my kids for most of their professional lives" (p. 26).

In an *incompetent system,* the answer to "Is this the best?" cannot get beyond what teachers and administrators believe to be the limitations of the system. These limitations are created and sustained because staff feel that "this is the way things are" regardless of their individual satisfaction with the status quo. This doesn't mean that change is impossible in an incompetent system. Staff development workshops and opportunities can be plentiful in these systems. What is lacking, however, is clarity about how an innovation relates to why we are here, how one innovation relates to another, or how one innovation has a ripple effect on other elements of a school. One possible sign of an incompetent system is when teachers or administrators resoundingly complain that this innovation is "yet another thing that we have to do." A second sign is that staff believe that they can twist what they are already doing to "look like" they have made a change to their core practices when, in reality, they are simply conducting business as usual. "Compliance is not tantamount to acceptance" (Rossman, Corbett, & Firestone, 1988, p. 130). A third sign is that when the status quo is challenged, staff response tends to be fast, ferocious, and widespread. In fact, staff members tend to function most collegially and effectively when they are acting in solidarity against change.

In a *competent system,* teachers and administrators are constantly asking the question, "Is this the best way to achieve our purpose as a school?" and are committed to actively seeking out the answers through conversation and action research. This recursive inquiry is grounded in facts instead of feelings. This makes "behavioral change . . . possible through frequent communication of new definitions of what is and ought to be and close enforcement of these expectations" (Rossman, Corbett, & Firestone, 1988, p. 128). In a competent system, staff members clearly understand what is expected and take actions consistent with these expectations. In turn, administrators support such actions and model expectations.

Defining the Terms

The flowchart in Figure 2.1 illustrates the conceptual framework of both an incompetent and a competent system. Two phrases in Figure 2.1—"core beliefs" and "habitual practices"—merit special attention. They are essential to understanding competent and incompetent systems. A participant in either system might define them as follows:

➤ *Core beliefs* are immutable beliefs that define my purpose as an educator. They are who I am professionally. "Group members cannot even conceive of functioning in alternatives. . . ." (Rossman, Corbett & Firestone 1988, p. 125). When my core beliefs are met, I feel good about the work I do and the place where I do it. When I perceive that they are threatened, I resist, fight, and rarely change or give in totally.

➤ *Habitual practices* define what I do. They are the way I act or behave. I assume they allow me to put my core beliefs into operation. They "can be widely accepted as definitions of what is good and true, and yet group members also can be open to changing these expectations for behavior" (Rossman, Corbett, & Firestone, 1988, p. 125). When I

2.1

Conceptual Framework of an Incompetent System and a Competent System

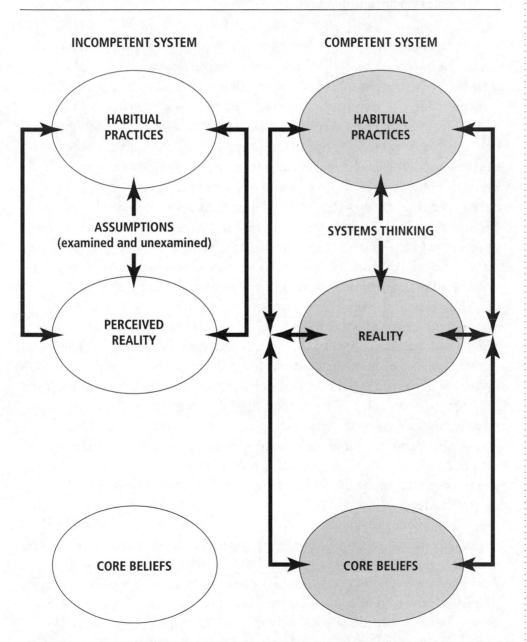

INCOMPETENT SYSTEM

COMPETENT SYSTEM

HABITUAL
PRACTICES

HABITUAL
PRACTICES

ASSUMPTIONS
(examined and unexamined)

SYSTEMS THINKING

PERCEIVED
REALITY

REALITY

CORE BELIEFS

CORE BELIEFS

➤

perceive that habitual practices are threatened, I will resist a change but will entertain it as an alternative when it shows promise for better achieving what I hold dear.

Picture a debate within a middle school faculty about integrating character education into every teacher's curriculum. The debate will be around such issues as "Whose job is that? Isn't that the job of the guidance counselor?" "You are taking time away from my class, and there are enough interruptions as is." The intent is to protect the status quo, to argue that the habitual practices are "good and true." The outcome tends to be determined by who holds the power, or, worse, who makes the most noise. Only when the system's core beliefs (or purpose) are clear and introduced into the conversation can the decision become one based on rational inquiry and not emotion. Is the purpose to "first serve the discipline we teach" or "to provide a safe, secure environment in which students can define themselves"? Only when the question is framed by the purpose can a change in behavior win strong staff support. It is this kind of conversation that engenders systems thinking.

The words of the third operating principle of this chapter—*Every staff member must be regarded as a trusted colleague in the examination of assumptions and habitual practices*—were carefully chosen to reinforce the point that a "trusted colleague" is one who is willing to see the "reality" of the system instead of relying on assumptions (perceived reality). This definition implies that disagreement will be a predictable part of collegiality. What keeps the relationship collegial is the trust each person has in the others to think through positions in light of the system's complexity and purpose. This operating principle confirms the value of the examination and also confirms that its validity depends on the open examination of the facts by all staff, not just designated leaders.

A competent system requires constant conversation among trusted colleagues about how to better achieve the system's purpose. The conversation is defined in terms of both the nature and the content of the discourse. For example, in a competent system, when a teacher teaches a lesson in a way that has always worked in the past but finds it isn't working for a particular group of students, he discusses the problem at his team-level meeting. The topic is not the competence of the teacher or the competence of the students;

the topic is the appropriateness of the lesson design. The intent is to get to the root of the problem and to consider how solutions to this particular problem could inform instructional practices of other teachers. The quality of the conversation's content and the collegiality of the relationships that allows it to take place are hallmarks of a competent system. In an incompetent system, the teacher would be reluctant to raise the issue at a team meeting out of concern about how he will be perceived by his colleagues.

Moving from an Incompetent to a Competent System

It takes a substantial amount of time, patience, tolerance, and resources to make these conversations productive. But even in the early stages of this approach, administrators and teachers begin to see the school as a complex, living system that is always evolving.

> We anticipate [the] evolution by asking questions like "Why is the system this way? Why do these rules exist? What is the purpose of this practice?" . . . Since we are part of the system ourselves we are drawn to inquire more deeply, to look for ways that our own assumptions and habitual actions are integral to creating the system as it operates today. Constantly questioning becomes a way of life.
> (Senge et al., 2000, pp. 55–56)

Figure 2.2 highlights some key differences between incompetent and competent systems. As the figure indicates, unexamined assumptions play a dominant role in an incompetent system, whereas critical examination characterizes a competent system. The challenge for Joan, Maria, Rob, and Susan is to bring assumptions to the surface for display and inquiry. They must work as colleagues and be prepared to "explore assumptions from new angles . . . and try to understand where they came from" (Senge et al., 2000, p. 76). They must each be willing to address the following questions:

➤ Can I express my assumptions clearly and then join in examining them without becoming defensive?
➤ Can I hear and accept others looking at my assumptions from different perspectives, perhaps even critical ones?

➤ Can I see common beliefs shaping all of the perspectives?

➤ Can I put my assumptions aside, if only for a while, and look at the school from the perspective of others?

➤ Can we as a group of colleagues develop new insights about our school after the uncovering, questioning, and testing of assumptions regarding how we do things?

2.2

Key Differences Between Incompetent and Competent Systems

INCOMPETENT SYSTEM	COMPETENT SYSTEM
Assumptions are based on **perceived reality**. Educators seem resigned (for better or for worse) that "this is the way things are" when they think about the reality of their classroom, their students, their working conditions, this staff, these teachers. Educators still examine their habitual practices, but their answer to "Is this best?" is always confined within the boundaries of what they assume to be feasible (which generally is a pessimistic view).	Systems thinking is based on **reality** ("what is") so that stakeholders can then determine "what can be." Instead of wishing away reality or obscuring certain elements of it, educators embrace "problems as friends" to determine what change is necessary, how that change will affect other elements of the system, and how the change will better enable all educators to satisfy their core beliefs.
Educators make **assumptions** that the habitual practice is the best (most appropriate) way of meeting their core belief. • When making **unexamined assumptions**, educators assume that "this is the best" practice or belief based on faith, habit, or familiarity. • When making **examined assumptions**, educators have asked the question, "Is this the best?" and have arrived at an answer that they believe is best in light of their core beliefs and their perceived reality.	Educators adhere to the operating principle that each school is a unique and complex living system with purpose. Therefore, teachers and administrators apply **systems thinking**; they are constantly examining the elements of the system to contemplate the whole, interrelate the various elements, discern the patterns, and think through how to redesign the patterns for learning and growth. Assumptions are short-lived in a competent system because there is constant critical examination of established practices to determine how (and if) they serve the core beliefs.

Staff Conversation #2

As Joan, Maria, Rob, and Susan begin their meeting, they are not consciously thinking about assumptions they carry about the school, the way it is managed, and the importance of controls in their working lives. However, as they begin talking, such assumptions surface and become the basis for further inquiry and insight.

Joan: I hope the opening of school has gone well.

Casual conversation follows for a few minutes. Rob raises the issue of existing assessment practices.

Rob: While all seems to be going well, teachers, including me, are doing what we do every year, concentrating on our own classrooms. I'm just waiting for the day when I have to meet with Carolyn, Miguel, and Sarah to discuss the midyear assessment. We'll be all over the place.

Joan: I thought that teachers did a good job coming together to create the core assessments. They've been in place for two years now and seem to have provided common expectations for teacher instruction and student learning.

Susan: I thought that the work on the math assessments went very well.

Rob: But assessments in math are a lot easier to design together than assessments in social studies. We get so bogged down in what's important in social studies that we never get around to agreeing on what should be covered on a common assessment, let alone how to evaluate it.

Joan: Why?

Maria: As far as I'm concerned, you could never get the group of teachers working together on the social studies core assessments to agree on anything. I'm happy that I'm the science coordinator. The physical science teachers work together, the life science teachers work together, and the earth science teachers work together.

Rob: And that's better? You sound as fragmented as the teachers working on social studies. Except you all have agreed to stay in your separate corners while we at least went a couple of rounds together. *[Laughing at the mental picture]* I can't even imagine what it must look like at the district level.

Maria: I resent the fact that you lump the work in science in with the rest of the school. I take a lot of pride in the work we've done.

Joan: But when I meet with the curriculum coordinators to complete a given task, we work until we achieve real consensus. I assume that's what the coordinators do in their work with staff. Wasn't that true with the common core subject area assessments?

Susan: Just to assure you, we've done very well in developing common midyear and end-of-year assessments. Last June, we even sat down together before giving the assessment to the kids and crossed off questions that we didn't all get to during the year. That way no kids were at a disadvantage. Teachers were so supportive of each other and came to agreement so readily.

Maria: Well, how is that better? Isn't the purpose of the core assessment to regulate what the teacher teaches? Your collective efforts to be fair actually put students at a disadvantage. A teacher who conscientiously kept pace in order to "finish" and a teacher who slowed down the pace to work more extensively on certain concepts with certain students are treated the same.

Rob: My group avoided that whole problem by building flexibility into the assessments. We each designed different parts, but each part differentiated instruction by asking students to complete one of four choices.

Susan: Is that still a core assessment? Sounds like four separate ones housed on one piece of paper.

Rob: Well, that was easier than putting up with an endless, ugly fight over who wins and who loses.

Joan: But don't you think that, since it was made a schoolwide innovation, it has changed how you work together?

Maria: I don't mean to be defensive, but at least I got teachers to work together. Do you really think that the curriculum coordinators collaborate? They're polite in your meetings, but then they go back and run things the way they always have. Think about the war you created when you decided to move to a new schedule. You never achieved consensus on that one; you just went ahead and did what you wanted to do over our objections.

Rob: Ouch! You hit a hot one.

Joan: Haven't we gotten over that war? It seems that we would have moved on by now.

Maria: But that war was all over the school, and the scars from three years ago are still with us.

Susan: I always resented the fact that, as a new teacher in the building during that time, I was pulled into an old war over a dead issue. This is what drags down the school and drags me down during faculty meetings. When was the last time we were all on the same page? It seems like every innovation creates as many problems as it does opportunities.

Joan: Maybe that's why we're all here.

Joan quietly observes that the tone and scope of the meeting seem to have gone way out of bounds. Everyone seems on edge and uncomfortable now, and Joan wonders how a meeting that was supposed to be a discussion of the future got so embroiled in the past. She looks for a transition back to more level-headed ground but isn't sure quite how to get there.

Analysis of Staff Conversation #2

Joan's seemingly benign surmise that staff recognize the value of collaboration in their work on core assessments leads to an unpredictable exchange about what collaboration looks like in different teams and how teachers feel about the quality of that work. Rather than such conflict being a hindrance to conversation and learning, it can be a positive sign about the health of the system. "People in [a professional learning] community are relentless in questioning the status quo, seeking new methods, testing those methods, and then reflecting on the results. Not only do they have an acute sense of curiosity and openness to new possibilities, they also recognize that the process of searching for answers is more important than having an answer. Furthermore, their search is a collective one" (DuFour and Eaker, 1998, p. 25–26).

Although difficult conversations about current inadequacies can be a powerful opportunity, they require true collegiality among the participants in order to stay focused on purpose as opposed to the personalities and past histories involved. To assume that all parties come to the table with such respect and recognition is problematic. Joan's responsibility at this point in the conversation is not to suppress the conflicts that have arisen but instead to facilitate the group's capacity to push below the surface of the conversation, critically address assumptions, examine more systemic problems, and clearly articulate purpose.

Staff Conversation #2 (continued)

Pondering the conversation so far, Joan recognizes that the teachers are immersed in past history and persisting conflicts. Yet, they also are beginning the process of systems thinking: surfacing and questioning assumptions and defining problems. But now Joan forcefully refocuses the discussion back to the original reason for the meeting.

Joan: When I was sitting in the office before scheduling this meeting, I was listing past innovations and trying to find some common elements among them. One of the common elements was assessment of student performance, which relates directly to what we've been discussing about core assessments.

Rob: If you think our discussion about core assessments creates problems, it gets much worse if you look at how teachers have different expectations for grading, class participation, attendance, homework, students working together, reading and writing assignments, use of correct grammar, etc., etc., etc.

Maria: Well, the only way to fix those problems would be to agree to a common set of expectations for students in the building. Like what a good class participant looks like . . . or what it means to "be prepared" for class. I think I'm talking about a rubric for these things—one rubric we would all use.

Susan: It's more than that, though. We as teachers are working in isolation. We fail to communicate with each other about how we teach, what we expect of students, and how we assess them. I think we've lost sight of my purpose for going into teaching: holding all students accountable for high achievement.

Joan: From what I'm hearing, it seems that we have a choice: to return to our core belief in rigor and student accountability and to address the problems around assessing student performance, or to allow our belief to be sacrificed while we continue as is. But as Maria's comment implied, the first option will lead us to talk about scoring student work and behavior against a shared rubric applied equitably across the classes. It strikes me that, if we go there, we're also talking about how we grade students and the form in which we report student achievement.

Maria: Are you suggesting that we should address all these problems? I'm not even sure we define achievement in the same way.

Rob: Far be it from me to sound cautious about rigor and accountability or the need for some wide-ranging changes, but wouldn't it be smart to start small and take one issue at a time?

Susan: That makes sense to me, but we have to get teachers working together on whatever we do. Which leads to a thought: teachers need more help on how to develop and grade good performance assessments.

Rob: Please, I hope you're not asking for another education guru to come teach us how to do our job.

Susan: No, I was thinking more about tapping teachers in the school who are skilled in developing performance assessments and using rubrics, teachers who see performance assessment as more rigorous.

Joan: I like this. I know some teachers who might be willing to share their work on assessment.

Maria: This sounds good, but I don't know if we're ready for all this. Which teachers are going to get in front of their colleagues and boast about how good they are? Also, when have teachers in this school ever really shared what they do? And if they did, who would adopt other teachers' practices, no matter how good they are?

Susan: But isn't this all the more reason why we have to do something? After all, we all agree on rigor and accountability; we're only looking at performance assessment as a way of better doing what we believe so deeply in.

Rob: I'd be willing to tell some of my colleagues that they don't know how best to assess and grade kids' performance in a fair and equitable way. Doesn't a kid have the right to know what excellence means and not find that it differs depending on the idiosyncratic definition of a particular teacher?

Maria: But what good is confronting our colleagues on so many topics going to do?

Joan: I'm not sure where we're going with this, but it does seem clear that we have some issues around assessing student performance that need addressing, issues that will have a profound effect on so many things we do and take for granted in the school. If we are to move forward as a school, we have to come to grips with them.

Rob: No doubt it has potential, but I have yet to see people in this building work well together.

Joan: What do you think the four of us are doing right now?

Rob: I'm having a good time, but so far all talk, no action.

Susan: But Joan, I like what you said about moving forward as a school. The most important thing that we can do is to get everybody to reaffirm our purpose and think collectively as a total school, critically examining all that we do.

Maria: Despite my doubts about what we can do, it seems that we're finally having a frank discussion about some real educational issues.

Rob: Wow! I just looked at my watch. We've been here for almost two hours. I have to go, but let's continue this.

Maria: I'm up for that too. This is refreshing for an old-timer like me.

Joan: I want the four of us to continue this conversation. Susan suggested that we focus attention on how to help teachers develop good performance assessments. And there's still the issue of inconsistencies in how we assess student performance throughout the school. In our next meeting, we can develop some concrete plans for further action around assessment of students.

Maria: I'm a little nervous about the complexity of all we've talked about, but I definitely want to be here for that discussion.

Rob: So do I.

Susan: If this all leads to our moving forward as a school.

Joan: Thanks for your support.

Analysis of Staff Conversation #2

This conversation establishes common ground for Joan and her teachers to consider continuous improvement from a systems perspective, perhaps for the first time together in their careers. What made this common ground possible was that Joan created the opportunity for the conversation, "a free exploration that brings to the surface the full depth of people's experience and thought, and yet can move beyond their individual views" (Senge, 1990, pp. 239, 241). A shared process is emerging: the envisioning of what is wanted. It is the gap between what *is* and what *can be* that propels the move to planning and action.

To sustain this conversation over time, Joan must continue to show (through her words and her actions) that she sees her conversations with teachers as a mutual quest. However, it is important to keep in mind that this will be a difficult process:

> Members of a professional learning community must be prepared to slosh around together in the mess, to endure temporary discomfort, to accept uncertainty, to celebrate their discoveries, and to move quickly beyond their mistakes. They must recognize that even with the most careful planning, misunderstandings will occur occasionally, uncertainty will prevail, people will resort to old habits, and things will go wrong." (DuFour and Eaker, 1998, p. 283)

The messiness of this process becomes easier to tolerate when the collegiality becomes a shared search for the best means to achieve a deeply valued, shared purpose.

Principal Reflection #3

In a follow-up memo to the three teachers, Joan reiterates the objective established at the end of the last meeting:

> To develop some concrete plans for further action toward better achieving our parallel purposes of rigor and student accountability through more effective assessment of student performance.

But as she attempts to outline an agenda for the meeting, she finds that the objective is both vague and complex. Why did I say "some" plans rather than one? Isn't it better to have one plan to bring the total faculty together? But isn't more than one plan better to accommodate different needs? And what about "concrete"? It sounds nice to be concrete, but are four of us going to outline concrete plans for other teachers without their input? And don't the plans need to be more complete so that the staff is clear on the direction of the conversation? And what about "action"? Don't we need other conversations within the school to get others on board before we act? And finally, "assessment of student performance"—the last meeting left me with the impression that the school is all over the place on this. Performance assessment seems to be a beginning focal point, but what if teachers keep harping on the point that we do not have common standards about any-thing—from attendance to student writing? If I bring all these questions to the table with Maria, Rob, and Susan, we may well have another two-hour meeting without any real sense of accomplishment. How often will these three teachers come back to the table if we simply have endless conversations about school problems?

Her reflection prompts a series of questions about Maria, Rob, and Susan. After long years of service, has Maria become cynical and thus a hindrance to change? Or is she frankly expressing observations that reflect the reality of the school? Is Rob able to move beyond his successes in the classroom and his critical view of colleagues to consider sustained collaborative efforts to pro-duce a better school? What is a "better school"? What is student achieve-ment? Does Susan really understand the complexities of this school enough to help in a process that is going to involve some careful, critical deliberation about what can work and how? In raising these questions, Joan realizes that she could ask these questions about any member of the school community, including herself.

The upcoming meeting is becoming far more complicated than Joan had anticipated. She begins to appreciate the barrage of questions that dominate her thinking and to see them as opportunities to interrelate different elements to create change within the school. With this in mind, she formulates a set of questions and attempts to draw interconnections among them to frame a plan.

➤ Where do we want our school to be? Is it enough to say that we want rigor and student accountability? Are there more core beliefs that must be brought to the surface and made explicit? How do these beliefs relate to achievement?

➤ What makes our school what it is? What are its elements and how do they interrelate? Are there patterns in these relationships?

➤ Why should assessment of student performance be the place to start staff development? What makes it so important to us?

➤ What is there about performance assessment that can move us forward as a learning organization?

➤ Where do the opportunities exist in the school for continuous school improvement around assessment of student performance?

➤ What are the barriers to continuous school improvement? How can we overcome them?

➤ What do we have to know about our school for continuous improvement to work? How can we change the patterns in our school for effective action?

➤ Whom else do we have to get on board as a next step?

Summing Up and Looking Ahead

A competent system is grounded in the school as a complex living system with purpose. It is through systems thinking and collegial conversation that administrators and teachers begin the process of critically analyzing assumptions that perpetuate the status quo, recognizing previously unseen complexities and conflicts within the school, welcoming problems as friends, and perceiving the gaps between what is and what can be. For the school to have purpose, members of the school community must identify their core beliefs and develop a shared vision. Once these are established, staff development can become purposeful and systemic.

Joan's next step: She must now lead by working with key stakeholders to identify the school's core beliefs and to develop the shared vision.

Maria, Rob, and Susan's next step: They must decide whether to commit to working with Joan in these efforts, freely offering their perspectives to ensure that the vision is shared and that it provides a coherent picture.

The reader's next step: With your school and your district in mind, consider the following questions:

➤ Is the principal the instructional leader? If not, who is?

➤ What is "building leadership"? Is it the same as management? Should it be?

➤ Are there issues of trust that get in our way? What are they? Where are they? Where is trust strongest? Why? Are there experiences here that we can use to address a lack of trust in other areas? What are these experiences? How can we use them?

➤ What do we believe? What beliefs are most important? For how many? How do we know? Is our evidence valid and reliable?

➤ As we explore change, do we have standards for judging the effectiveness of any approach? Do we use the standards? How often? What is the evidence?

➤ Do we explore current practice against a set of standards? Do we use the standards consistently? Regularly? What's the standard? What's the evidence?

➤ Are school beliefs and district beliefs in agreement? If so, can staff articulate those beliefs? If not, can the differences be negotiated?

➤ Can we talk with one another? About what? Are there patterns here?

➤ It's tough stuff. Do we have the will and the energy to do it? Who does? Who doesn't? Does any difference in who does and who doesn't matter? Why?

ENVISIONING THE DESIRED RESULTS

Essential Questions

What beliefs define our purpose? How do we know them when we see them?

Operating Principles

– A shared vision articulates a coherent picture of what the school will look like when the core beliefs have been put into practice.

– The legitimacy of a shared vision is based on how well it represents all perspectives in the school community.

Chapter Overview

This chapter focuses on how our fictional school moves through the first two steps of continuous improvement: identifying and clarifying core beliefs and establishing a shared vision. The purpose of every school is to optimize student achievement; it is the core beliefs that define achievement.

The first step, identifying and clarifying the core beliefs, requires sustained conversation among representatives of all members of the school community. Although individuals achieve consensus on what the core beliefs should be, that consensus will likely collapse when it comes to describe what those beliefs look like in practice. These steps begin the journey toward collective autonomy and provide the framework for a competent system, which includes purposeful staff development.

The second step of continuous improvement then must produce the shared vision of the school: a coherent picture of how the system will function when the core beliefs have been put into practice. It is only when the school has a shared vision that administrators and staff can determine the gaps between what *is* and what *should be* and proceed toward purposeful staff development that nurtures and advances a competent system.

This chapter also introduces a new character: Henry, the district superintendent. He is an experienced administrator but is relatively new to the district. He is known for the importance he assigns to data (most notably the scores on state assessments), which was one of the reasons he was hired. The board has given him a clear mandate that the district as a whole must pay closer attention to state standards.

Setting the Agenda

Principal Reflection #4

Joan drives out of the Board of Education parking lot with her fists clenched around the steering wheel. A car horn blasts at her from behind, an impatient reminder that the light has just turned green. Her first meeting of the year with Henry has left Joan feeling anxious about her tentative efforts to reach out to staff to improve the quality of teaching and learning. She emphasized the value of conversation with staff about how staff development could be better aligned with their needs; he emphasized the necessity to improve student academic performance and sustain the achievement over time. Henry acknowledged her need to exercise more instructional leadership in the building but also insisted that such efforts be data-driven and tied to academic achievement (not dictated by the agendas of individual teachers). The remainder of the meeting was somewhat of a blur for Joan: the words "improve academic achievement" triggered a cacophony of voices in Joan's mind—irate parents, belligerent newspaper reporters, and morally outraged legislators—all demanding to know why the quality of learning wasn't better.

Joan makes it back to the school in time for the dress rehearsal of the fall play where she struggles to keep her internal conversation from drowning out the student dialogue on stage. She considers calling Ed during the intermission but does not want him to know how uncomfortable she feels. Although he is a valued colleague, she remains keenly aware of the bureaucratic hierarchy that separates them.

It isn't until Joan is on her way back to school the following morning that she begins to recall other pieces of yesterday's conversation with the superintendent.

> ➤ Henry emphasized looking at state test scores over time, building capacity within schools to make high academic achievement a reality, and focusing the attention of the entire district on teaching and learning in the classroom, resulting in student achievement and success as he felt they should be defined.

> ➤ He mentioned a presentation by Richard Elmore on strategic thinking that left him feeling committed to the need to drive all thinking in a district toward what happens in the classroom (Lecture, National Staff Development Council Annual Conference, 9 December 2002).

> ➤ He emphasized that he and the assistant superintendent had to rely on the principals as the key links between the district office and the classroom, bringing the message to teachers that their work is essential to enhanced student performance and success.

Anxious about following through on her train of thought before getting lost in the details of the day, Joan sits at her desk and sketches out a Venn diagram to compare her own beliefs about the direction of the work in her building and the key points Henry made at their meeting (see Figure 3.1). As she begins shading in the intersection of the two circles with her pencil, the answer suddenly clicks. She writes in big block letters in the intersection: "ACADEMIC ACHIEVEMENT."

Analysis of Principal Reflection #4

Joan's epiphany may appear somewhat unremarkable; but, in fact, it is an important step in the development of her own personal vision of her work as school principal. If she decides that academic achievement is a top priority,

---

3.1

Finding the Intersection of Joan's and Henry's Agendas

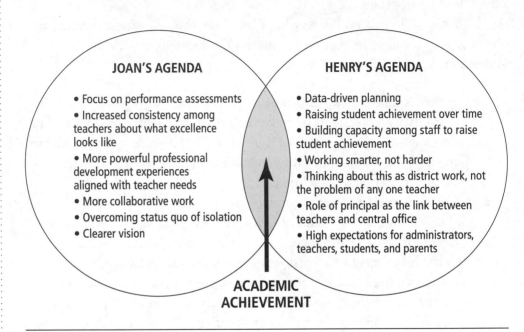

JOAN'S AGENDA

- Focus on performance assessments
- Increased consistency among teachers about what excellence looks like
- More powerful professional development experiences aligned with teacher needs
- More collaborative work
- Overcoming status quo of isolation
- Clearer vision

HENRY'S AGENDA

- Data-driven planning
- Raising student achievement over time
- Building capacity among staff to raise student achievement
- Working smarter, not harder
- Thinking about this as district work, not the problem of any one teacher
- Role of principal as the link between teachers and central office
- High expectations for administrators, teachers, students, and parents

ACADEMIC ACHIEVEMENT

---

how would that change her current allocation of time, energy, and resources? Would she undertake the following steps?

➤ Allocate curriculum development funds to create stronger alignment between state standards and targeted processes and "big ideas" in teacher-generated curriculum.

➤ Research best practices for assessment both among staff and in education literature to determine how to gain more reliable data about the depth of student understanding.

➤ Evaluate how teachers diversify instruction to help all students engage in the learning process.

➤ Work with parents to make sure they are informed about key dates for assessments (both locally created and state mandated) as well as other related issues, including assessment structure, content focus, their role in their child's learning, and support available.

To transform a school community, a vision must be shared. Joan must not only reframe her own work to pursue this new agenda, but also engage other key stakeholders in the same endeavor. As Senge et al. (2000) suggests,

> Suppose there were ways for all of them to talk together—not once, but repeatedly, starting from the assumption that they all had the best interests of the school and its children in mind. Then the school system could begin to shift from a complex set of interlocked but separate constituencies to a body of people who were learning together, on behalf of their common purpose. (p. 272)

To move forward on this idea, Joan once again will need to reach out to critical friends. But this time the net will have to be cast much wider. She needs people (from all key groups—parents, community members, staff, students) who have a picture about what the school is, what it ought to be, and how to make it better. She needs a focus group.

The purpose of putting together a focus group is to move all participants from their individual roles as stakeholders (individual autonomy) to a common role of shared responsibility (collective autonomy).

➤ *Individual autonomy* is a mode of operation in which people generally work alone in pursuit of self-defined goals and interests because they see no pressing need to serve the system and its purposes. The school as a system becomes a loose confederation that houses individual efforts within separate environments. Individual autonomy reigns in an incompetent system; individuals assume that they can accomplish more working alone than with others and that the system is there primarily to support their individual efforts.

➤ *Collective autonomy* is a mode of operation in which people generally collaborate in pursuit of shared goals and interests that serve the individual and the system. The school as a system becomes a united body in its determination to achieve the desired results but still fosters open inquiry and individual creativity. Collective autonomy is a hallmark of a competent system. A competent system proves itself when everyone within the system performs better as a result of the collective endeavors and accepts accountability for that improvement (this is an operating principle discussed in Chapter 7).

To move from individual autonomy to collective autonomy, stakeholders must engage in collegial conversations about the school, its purpose, its beliefs, and its problems. As discussed in Chapter 2, this kind of conversation is not free from debate or disagreement. Stakeholders will come to appreciate that these analytic (and often difficult) conversations are the only way to continuously examine whether a habitual practice is the best way to achieve the shared vision of the school. The following conversation illustrates the ability of teachers to learn to become systems thinkers. These teachers always had the potential for systems thinking, but the daily realities of their jobs left this potential unrealized or untapped. Although the three teachers continue to ask pointed questions in this conversation, they also are becoming more intrigued by the pursuit of the answers.

Staff Conversation #3

Although Joan is ready to broaden the scope of the group, she wants to honor the relationship that she has established with the three teachers. They reconvene to brainstorm how to get a conversation going among a larger group. Joan poses four questions to the teachers:

1. Whom are we going to invite?
2. Who should facilitate the focus group?
3. How will this focus group meeting be set up?
4. What will the group actually be discussing?

Question #1: Whom are we going to invite?

Susan: Well, we definitely need to have teachers there. And administrators.

Rob: Done. Next question?

Maria: Not so fast! Don't we need to ask the students too? If our students are too young, what about former students? I mean, we're talking about their achievement, and they're an important part of the learning that goes on in the classroom.

Rob: Well, I could argue that their parents know more about the learning in the classroom than the students do. They probably value the learning process more than their kids do.

Joan: I think we have to have parents there too.

Rob: Why not just invite everybody, then? Board members, business leaders, community politicians, newspaper reporters . . .

Joan: I actually think we should.

Maria: Goodness knows, all those people have opinions on what we're doing. For once we can have the conversations around the same table instead of around our separate dinner tables.

They decide that the focus group will be made up of 20 to 25 participants who embody the diversity of the community and the school staff along age, experience, racial, ethnic, and socioeconomic lines. After more conversation, they also agree that the focus group must reflect other types of diversity: parents heavily involved in school activities as well as those who have never attended a school event; students with a variety of learning needs and a variety of achievement levels; teachers with a range of experience with students in various settings and program areas. Each participant will be invited because he or she can wear multiple hats; for example,

- A teacher who is a team leader and also vice president of the local teachers association;
- A member of the board who also has children in the district and participates in her school's parent teacher association;
- A student who is on the student council and is in a variety of levels of academic classes;
- A community member who is editor of the local newspaper as well as coach of his daughter's parks department soccer team.

This tactic will keep the group size manageable and will encourage each participant to represent a variety of perspectives.

Analysis of Staff Conversation #3

Rob's concern about the size of the group is a powerful reminder that these kinds of conversations around deep beliefs about education don't happen often.

> Perhaps the most significant thing we have learned is the importance of respectful involvement of all stakeholders . . . .Without their involvement, our visions become mandates without meaning. Our stakeholders feel discounted and marginalized. The result is a lack of understanding and commitment from those whose support we need the most. (Brown & Moffett, 1999, p. 87)

The status quo in this building, and in many others, has been that parents and teachers work together on organizational and communication issues (start of the school day, new format for progress reports, funding for extracurricular activities, and so on). It is assumed that "we're all doing this for the kids," but parents and teachers never really get to think through or explicitly define the underlying beliefs that drive their mutual efforts. In many instances, it would seem inconceivable to have this conversation, especially with students in the room. At the same time, these conversations must respect the existing roles that constitute the school community so that everyone feels involved while keeping the boundaries of their individual and collective responsibilities somewhat intact.

Staff Conversation #4

Question #2: Who should facilitate the focus group?

The group quickly agrees that because of the range of perspectives around the table, it is essential to have a skilled facilitator who is committed to soliciting a range of responses.

Susan: This isn't going to be an easy task, considering that parents, teachers, community leaders, and administrators rarely sit down and have this kind of conversation about our system.

Rob: Do you think people are going to be able to stop walking on eggshells with each other? The real conversation will happen only if people move beyond their roles and believe they're all after the same thing.

Maria: I thought the point of having a focus group was because of the diversity of roles. Don't we want the conversation to reflect the range of perspectives? I think it would be worse to have a generic conversation about learning without any grounding in personal experience with the system, whatever that personal experience looks like.

Susan: But what about Rob's point about people being so afraid of offending each other that they never really say what they think? We can't have a conversation if people are too timid to say what's really on their minds.

Joan: Remember, we already decided that we're committed to having a range of perspectives in these focus groups. I think we will be okay if we have participants play multiple roles and if our facilitator is clear about the need to honor all perspectives and avoids getting bogged down by any single participant's agenda.

After brainstorming a list of staff members and others who might be interested, willing, and able to take on the task of facilitator, the group arrives at four names: Ed, the assistant superintendent; Maria (who volunteered herself); Sylvia, the school guidance counselor (who works with a range of the students, staff, and parents on a daily basis); and Carmen, parent of a former student and past secretary of the parent teacher association (who not only has had training as a facilitator but also served as a parent representative on the school's now defunct School Improvement Team). After some animated discussion about the positive qualities of these people, the group decides that all of them should be invited to the focus group and that Carmen should be asked to facilitate. The key is her training and experience as a focus group facilitator as well as her proven commitment to the school. As Joan makes a note to herself to call Carmen, Maria leans over to Joan and says, "Make it clear to Carmen that we've asked her to assume this role as a facilitator and not as a parent." Joan nods in agreement, and the planning continues.

Question #3: How will this focus group meeting be set up?

Susan: I don't want to leave Rob's concern just yet. I still think we can do more by design to make people more comfortable with one another. I know Carmen is capable, but we definitely need to establish the right tone ahead of time.

Rob: Well, for one thing, I think it would help if we all looked the same. Have a rule about what we wear so that some people don't show up in power suits and others show up in jeans.

Maria: Something else that would instantly make me feel more comfortable would be if we were not in a fishbowl like the glassed-in conference room in the main office. When people walk by, not only is it an instant distraction, but it also will make people less able to relax with one another. Face it, it's not normal in this system for these people to be around the table together.

Joan: But shouldn't it be? Isn't that what we're working toward?

Susan: Yes, but working toward a goal is very different from its being standard operating procedure. I think it would make more sense to meet off school grounds. Maybe one of the local businesses would donate their conference space. Or the town hall.

Joan: But again, I want to be clear. If we go off-site for these conversations, we have to be doing it for the right reasons. The wrong reason would be that we're afraid of how people would react to the fact that we're doing this.

Rob: Well, why would their reaction be bad if they know in advance that we're doing it? We're going to be telling people about it in advance, right?

Maria: You mean the focus group participants that we're inviting?

Rob: No. I actually mean everyone. I think that we should send out a letter, make announcements, ask for input, promise to share results the next day, and publicize the fact that we're taking this step so that we can talk about . . . hey, what are we actually talking about? I know that we said "our common beliefs about learning," but what exactly does that mean?

Question #4: What are we actually talking about?

Joan: Academic achievement and how we each think it happens right now and could happen more effectively.

Susan: And what our individual and collective responsibilities are in making that happen.

Maria: You know, is that what we're really about? Do you remember the point raised by the parent at the PTA meeting last month? That the purpose of school was to develop the whole child? Her son wasn't, in her words, "an academic student." What was the school going to do for him? How does the school meet the needs of students who aren't invested in the traditional sense but still deserve to be comfortable and competent in the domain of the school?

Rob: I guess we're raising another issue—whose school is it anyway?

Joan: I thought we figured it out already. Our job is to raise academic achievement. That's the best way we can meet the needs of all students, regardless of how they (or their parents) categorize them.

Maria: But aren't there people who believe that the emotional and social needs of their children are every bit as important as (and for some even more important than) academic achievement? There may be additional core beliefs that in the minds of participants are as valid and important as the one that we've already identified.

Analysis of Staff Conversation #4

It is important to pause in the conversation to acknowledge that what just happened could have undermined the integrity of the entire focus and planning process. Joan's individual struggle to get clarity on her work led to a series of dilemmas and insights about how to move from an incompetent to a competent system. Although her Venn diagram exercise earlier in the chapter solidified that improving academic achievement was a core belief, she then slipped back into "assumption mode" and assumed on behalf of all participants (before they even met) that they, too, held the same core belief. Articulation of the core beliefs, however, requires the participation of all members of the school community. Joan unintentionally violates this tenet even though she values the perspectives of others.

What is important to emphasize is that Joan is in the process of *becoming* part of a competent system. There are times when one slips back into old habits and patterns, and that is to be expected. It requires vigilance to catch these moments as they happen and to refocus as necessary. In this instance, it was Maria who recognized the slip and pointed it out to Joan, but in other instances, Joan catches herself and refocuses. Joan also points out slips that the teachers have made, and they, too, have refocused back on "the right things." What already is operating here is shared leadership to the extent that all participants are trusted colleagues in this process.

Staff Conversation #4 (continued)

Joan: Well, the question then becomes, "What do we really believe defines excellence in education?"

Maria: But how do we frame the conversation in a way that puts all participants on equal ground? If the question places too much responsibility in the domain of one group of stakeholders, it will quickly degenerate into a defensive conversation.

Susan: We need to take the core beliefs that come out of the conversation around the question of excellence and then ask, "How do we do whatever it is?"

Rob: And under what conditions? Tell me what you want, tell me how you'll know it, and then get out of my way and let me decide how best to do it.

Maria: What I'm hearing is that we need consensus among all stakeholders around the first two questions, but the way we put all of this into practice belongs in the domain of the professionals. Aren't we the ones who are responsible for making decisions about those conditions because we know what works and what doesn't? What's feasible and what isn't?

Susan: Based on what? Our professional two cents? Research? Current practice? I'm not sure that we understand these conditions better than the other stakeholders in the school community.

Joan: I just think it's too much too soon. You can't have parents, board members, etc., at every conversation without really making teachers defensive about the right to do their job without interference.

Analysis of Staff Conversation #4

Although Joan and the staff are beginning to take risks in what they say to each other, they have yet to extend the same level of trust to other key stakeholders. Trust, however, is key in this process. The focus group meeting that will soon take place is noteworthy as an example of parental and community involvement, but it has a definite lifespan: it is designed as a one-time event with a limited charge. Joan and the staff clearly have reservations about the extent of that involvement because they don't believe (at least right now) that these stakeholders should be regarded as equal players. The most troublesome example of this reservation is the side conversation between Maria and Joan about making sure Carmen knows her "place." It is interesting that Maria and Joan offhandedly discuss this as an obvious concern that can be easily handled by a pleasant phone conversation. Underlying this seemingly innocuous point is a concern about the ability of parents to be objective when it comes to the work of schools. Can they see beyond their own children? Although the story line will put this issue aside for much of the book, there are places where Joan and the staff need to continue to build trust beyond the walls of the school in a more consistent and open-ended manner.

After the meeting with Maria, Rob, and Susan, Joan goes back to her office and thinks about the various points they raised. She then composes an invitation to be sent to the people chosen to take part in the focus group, scheduled for four weeks later (see Figure 3.2).

The Focus Group Meeting

After welcoming and thanking everyone for volunteering their time, Carmen, the facilitator, quickly turns to the task at hand. After noticing that people are seated primarily in like clusters (parents, students, staff, community), she has the participants count off by fives and split into small groups according to their numbers. This creates six small groups that reflect a range of roles. She then asks each group to develop a response to the following question: *What do we really believe defines excellence in education?*

Although the participants are trying to do the task at hand, Joan is keenly aware of the tension and anxiety in the room. She pulls Carmen aside and

➤

3.2
Invitation to the Focus Group Meeting

An Invitation to Work Together

For school renewal to endure, every school and district . . . needs principles that transcend the interests of any individual and that are derived from constituents. . . . These principles comprise a covenant—a living embodiment of why we as a school community do what we do.

Carl Glickman, *Renewing America's Schools*

We are all concerned about excellence in education, but none of us alone is qualified to define that for the community. Your voice needs to be part of that examination so that the vision of the school honors the uniqueness of this community and the joint responsibility we share for ensuring the future of our young people.

We hope you will join us next month for a focus group discussion around the issue of excellence.

Date: Friday, November 2nd
Place: Meeting room in the public library
Time: 8:00 a.m.–5:00 p.m.

✔   Breakfast and lunch will be catered by a local restaurant.
✔   Please dress in casual and comfortable attire—jeans and sneakers are fine!

I will call you sometime next week to explain the purpose of the meeting, to identify what role you will play in the conversation, and to answer any questions you might have. I look forward to our next conversation.

Sincerely,

Joan Michaelson
School Principal

---

asks her if she should call a time-out to offer more clarification. Carmen tells her to be patient and let the conversation unfold; it takes time for people to become comfortable enough to disagree. Fifteen minutes later, the room is buzzing with conversation. Joan relaxes as she realizes that people have really begun to talk with one another, as opposed to simply making statements and adding them to their lists. After the small groups finish developing their brainstormed response to the question, Carmen guides them through a reporting process that results in one collective list. The next challenge is to take this extensive response and do something with it.

After a quick refreshment break, Carmen orients the group to their next task: *What patterns or themes begin to emerge? As you start to identify these, group the responses underneath them.*

As the patterns are reported back to the larger group, it becomes apparent that two core beliefs dominate the conversation:

> ➤ An excellent school must promote high academic achievement.
> ➤ An excellent school must ensure equity.

The next step is to flesh out what "high academic achievement" and "equity" look like in language that is both concrete and aligned with the values of the organization. Over lunch, Carmen, Joan, Maria, Rob, and Susan meet to debrief how the morning went and to project a direction for the afternoon. Based on the group's emphasis on academic achievement and equity, they decide it is now appropriate to pose the question, "How do students best learn?" They prepare directions to guide the response process (see Figure 3.3). In addition to the question on learning, they also decide that a separate question needs to be created to explore the group's beliefs about equity. "How do we best achieve equity?" By completing these tasks, a vision of what these core beliefs would look like begins to emerge.

The participants share dozens of recollections that afternoon. They then consolidate these highly personalized thoughts into a few key statements, including these examples:

> ➤ Students learn best when they can connect all the discrete pieces of knowledge they are learning. It is in the inference making that the learning takes place.
> ➤ Students learn best when they are curious. What engages them is a problem that they see as *worth* solving, one that is meaningful to them. This experience motivates them to ask questions and to plan strategies for solving the problem.

>

3.3
Focus Group Handout

How do students best learn?

STEP 1   Think back to your many prior experiences both in and out of school. What was the best learning experience you have ever encountered as a learner?

STEP 2   In sharing your recollections and analyses with the group, create a list of generalizations that follow from the accounts. What do these learning experiences have in common?

Source: Adapted from *Understanding by Design Handbook* (1999), by Grant Wiggins and Jay McTighe (Alexandria, VA: Association for Supervision and Curriculum Development).

> Students learn best when the purpose of their learning and the expectations for them are clear. They don't have to guess what they are supposed to learn or how well they are expected to learn it.

After generating their recollections and key statements on student learning, the participants move on to the next question: *How do we best achieve equity?* Carmen instructs the small groups to work directly with the question. Examples of the beliefs that arise out of the process include the following:

> We achieve equity best when we hold all students to the same high-quality standards.
> We achieve equity best when we ensure students have equal access to all learning opportunities.

Carmen reserves the last 20 minutes of the session to debrief what they learned and what still needs to be done. The participants are exhausted but pleased with the richness and depth of the conversation. However, some participants voice reservations about their ongoing roles in the envisioning process. One parent comments, "Everything we said made sense to me, and I really appreciate being part of the process to achieve consensus in our community around achievement and equity, but I don't know how much more I have to say than what I've said already." The editor of the local newspaper also expresses reservations about continuing the conversation, but for different reasons: "I think we've gained clarity based on our own prior knowledge and perspective, but it seems good practice at this point to compare our conclusions with those generated in the body of educational theory and research." One of the local business leaders offers another insight into the limitations of the conversation: "Don't we need to find out what the data show about how the school currently is honoring these beliefs about achievement and equity? It's really an issue of quality control, not just a wish list of what we hope to be."

The participants conclude that these tasks are more appropriately done by the school staff. Joan agrees to pick up the conversations back at the school and promises to keep the participants updated on the progress of the work. As she drives home that evening, she is keenly aware of the next conversations that must take place.

> ➤ She must report back to her staff the substance of the conversation as well as the next steps as recommended by the focus group and endorsed by her.
> ➤ She must update Henry on the focus group meeting and get his approval to develop a sustained staff development plan centered on academic achievement and equity. She is relieved that the focus group's core belief in academic achievement is in alignment with his and the other key policymakers' belief.

Analysis of the Focus Group Meeting

The focus group meeting has become a real opportunity for shared common interests to develop (Cook, 1986). The process is democratic in its articulation of the role of the school in achieving excellence.

During the conversation process, people learn how to think together—not just in the sense of analyzing a shared problem or creating new pieces of shared knowledge but in the sense of occupying a collective sensibility, in which the thoughts, emotions, and resulting actions belong not to one individual, but to all of them together. (Senge et al., 2000, p. 75)

The power of these conversations is that the stakeholders in the system have an opportunity to participate in the identification and clarification of core beliefs instead of simply being recipients of them. This is vital to the integrity of the shared vision because the "uniqueness" of the school is both a reflection and a product of all of the stakeholders.

Why is uniqueness important? Because creating a unique school and being part of a unique school helps us feel special and improves our level of commitment. Shared commitments pull people together and create tighter connections among them and between them and the school. And these factors count in helping students learn at higher levels. (Sergiovanni, 2000, p. 23)

The next step is to bring the conversation back to the full staff to determine the validity of the generalizations and to articulate a more precise picture of what these generalizations would look like if put into practice.

The Faculty Meeting

Joan calls a special faculty meeting for the following Tuesday afternoon to present both the scope of the focus group conversation and the statements of the two core beliefs necessary for school excellence. The fact that she is calling a special faculty meeting will not come as a surprise to her staff because she had already informed them about why she made the decision to call for a focus group, what the group would be charged with discussing, and how they could participate if they chose.

Joan first presents the initial findings of the focus group on a PowerPoint slide:

> ➤ An excellent school must promote high academic achievement.
> ➤ An excellent school must ensure equity.

After a few vague endorsements and a long, awkward pause, a teacher known for his directness says, "Who could argue with that?" Seeing many heads nod in agreement, Joan moves on to the next slide, which delineates the key beliefs about learning articulated at the focus group meeting. After reading through the findings, Joan once again opens up the meeting for reactions. Although staff members find the insights interesting, questions immediately arise about the validity of the generalizations for the whole school.

> ➤ *Are they more a reflection of individual learning experiences in a particular school in a particular place, or do they hold up as a generalization for all schools?*
> ➤ *Do these generalizations offer a complete picture?*
> ➤ *Does the list reflect the range of the participants who were there?*
> ➤ *Was the amount of time devoted to the activity sufficient?*
> ➤ *Would those generalizations change if another set of focus group participants were selected?*

Joan had anticipated that these kinds of questions might be raised, and she distributes a handout to lay out the next step in the envisioning process (see Figure 3.4). Amid the groans at the prospect of the sizable task at hand, teachers begin firing more questions at Joan.

Question: How are we going to find the time to get this done?

Joan: I have already adjusted the staff development schedule so that this is the agenda for the next several months until it is done. [*This school has early release one day per month for staff development work.*] In addition, I commit to allotting at least two-thirds of every faculty meeting to this work. You'll have to keep me informed if you need additional time.

Question: Why us? Can't you find some outside organization or consultant to do this?

Joan: The shared vision for this building has got to honor what is unique, what is special about this place. You know as well as, if not better than, anyone what the health of this system is and where we need to make improvements. You are assessors of where the students have been, guides for where they are going to go today, and a part of who they are going to become as learners tomorrow.

<table>
<tr><td colspan="2">3.4
Analysis Task for Developing the Shared Vision</td></tr>
<tr><td colspan="2">**How do students best learn? Under what conditions?**</td></tr>
<tr><td>**Goal**</td><td>To evaluate whether we have a comprehensive and measurable list that can guide the development of a shared vision for the system in support of our core beliefs on achievement and equity.</td></tr>
<tr><td>**Task**</td><td>Analyze the focus group's generalizations about learning through the lens of education theory and research.
1. Identify key sources (authors, periodicals, studies).
2. Sort, analyze, and synthesize information and data.
3. Summarize key findings and revise generalizations as needed.
4. Articulate shared vision based on each generalization and the findings.</td></tr>
</table>

Question: Then why turn outside of the school for information? Why not just collect data on what we are currently doing?

Joan: These are two separate sources of data, both of them valuable, but in very different ways. Once we're clear on what our vision for school excellence is, we then will audit our habitual practices to determine whether what we are currently doing is the most efficient, effective, and desirable method of achieving our core beliefs.

Question: What business is it of mine what happens outside of my classroom? I'm already overwhelmed just trying to do right by my kids. Although your idea sounds nice, I can't afford to be distracted by the work of the school.

Joan: We're all responsible to produce results with whatever students we have this year. But that responsibility doesn't end when the students move on to the next grade level or the next school. We're responsible to design learning experiences that fit into a larger scope of instruction that respects the fact that these students came from another teacher and are going to another. Even if you believe that you're doing exceptional work with them now, that work can unwittingly or deliberately be undone the following year. One of my hopes is that this envisioning process will bring us closer together in our practices and our beliefs. In fact, without this type of agreement, we can't claim to have a program across the grades.

Question: Does bringing us closer together mean that we will lose our independence? That's what makes this school and all schools great: an eclectic combination of pedagogy, passions, and philosophies on what will get students involved and invested in their own learning. You can hold us accountable to operate within the same framework (national, state, or local content standards), but aren't you crossing the line to ask us to have the same vision?

Joan: Before I answer this question, I want to acknowledge that I expect it will take time and many more conversations for us to all get to a place where this answer becomes standard operating procedure. I believe that, in successful schools, teachers and administrators do not have a lot of individual autonomy. Instead, educators exercise collective autonomy. Success comes from individual and group efforts to fulfill the group goals—high academic achievement and equity for all. Everyone, teachers and students alike, performs better as a result of the collective endeavor; the vision becomes a driving force for why we do what we do. Another piece of this, though, is that individual teachers embrace this kind of system as opposed to simply complying with it. If we consistently work together, starting today, to ask important questions, collect relevant research and data, work and talk together to analyze current practice, and brainstorm new possibilities, we can do better. We need to do better by our students and by ourselves.

Noting the time and sensing that interest is slipping away, Joan quickly wraps up the conversation. As she closes the meeting, she asks the staff to write down any additional questions they have on a slip of paper and put it in the basket on their way out the door.

Joan collects her things, picks up the basket, and looks through her purse to find the master key to lock the door. Out of the corner of her eye, she sees a slip of paper neatly folded on the top of the pile. Unable to resist curiosity, Joan unfolds the note to reveal a pointed but profoundly important statement and question: *Until today I thought I was doing a pretty good job. What's so wrong with what we're doing, and who we are, right now?*

Two months ago, this note might have thrown Joan off course and sent her back to her desk to adopt another one that would be more likely to safeguard the self-esteem of the staff. Instead, she surprises herself with her calm reaction and the ease with which she formulates an internal response: "This isn't about who you are as a professional; it's about who we are as a system. We don't even know who we are right now, because we haven't sat down and had the conversations to flesh that out. We've been doing the business of the school without looking at or thinking about where our standard operating procedures came from, let alone if they're working."

Administrator Conversation #2

The following day, Joan sits down with Henry, the superintendent, and Ed, the assistant superintendent, to update them on the focus group meeting and the staff response to both the focus group and their long-term task.

Henry: What are we going to see in this building when all of these things are in place?

Joan: When what is in place? The shared vision? A culture of collective autonomy?

Henry: You tell me. I want to know what indicators you will look to in order to gauge whether we're doing better in the areas of student achievement and equity. What are the baseline numbers you'll use for the comparison? What are the target numbers you hope to achieve? For example, are you looking to say that 75 percent of our students will be found competent on both the state and district assessments of student achievement after this vision has been implemented?

Joan: Well, which 25 percent are you willing to have incompetent? And would you give me their names because I'm sure their parents would like to know it.

Henry: Come on, Joan, that's not fair.

Joan: I appreciate the constant pressure on you, on all of us, to raise student achievement on the state assessment. However, this is only one indicator of excellence. If we're going to meet both of the core beliefs that have emerged, achievement and equity, then we have to ensure that our efforts to achieve the vision in one area don't undercut our efforts in another.

Henry: So what are you asking for? Permission to write a shared vision?

Joan: More than that. First, permission to write the shared vision with staff, with feedback from key stakeholders. Second, permission to use that vision as a means of identifying the kind of data we need to collect to see the degree to which we're honoring our beliefs. Third, permission to use the data to identify any gaps between practice and beliefs. And fourth, permission to do what is necessary to close those gaps, including action plans that will involve staff development.

Henry: I have to be honest with you. Right now I hear the value of what you're saying, but I want you to be very clear on two points. First, what you're saying in principle does not sound radical. What is radical, however, is that you think you can take this idea about collective autonomy and make it happen here. I admire your tenacity and your optimism, but, at the same time, I'm skeptical that you'll be able to change the culture of the building. Nevertheless, I won't let my skepticism stand in the way of your efforts. Second, I don't want you to lose sight of the fact that you are one school in a larger system. You're quite articulate on the need to have teachers function as systems thinkers within the scope of your organization, but I question whether you see your school as part of a larger system. I'm not going to write you a blank check to operate as if central office doesn't exist. There are other practices, other norms that you must adhere to regardless of what your staff concludes. For instance, this community is insisting upon accountability.

Ed: Joan and I have a well-established relationship that includes talking through those kinds of issues together, and I'm sure we'll continue to do so. I'm also sure that the process that Joan is following has merit for not only her staff but the entire system. I think it makes sense to let the process unfold in her building, keeping a close watch on what lessons we can learn for other buildings and what issues we need to be aware of to make sure that central office is working in conjunction with Joan and her staff as opposed to having them work in isolation.

Joan: I admit that I'm very school-centered and that it's fair to accuse me of the same self-centeredness that I'm trying to minimize in my own building.

There's a reasonable parallel between how teachers regard their students and how administrators regard their staff. We're fiercely dedicated to them above all other professional priorities. I hear you, and I promise that I'll communicate regularly with you and Ed to ensure that we evolve together.

Analysis of Administrator Conversation #2

This isn't an easy conversation for any of the administrators involved because it forces the issue of who is in control of the school. If the visioning process pulls people in Joan's building closer together as they work to make their core beliefs a reality, how does that affect the larger organization of schools? How closely aligned will the staff's commitments be with the commitments promulgated by district policy? How much in alignment should they be? Can (and should) the evolution of a school into a competent system drive the larger system in the same direction?

Joan, Ed, and Henry agree to "wait and see" before altering the scope of the innovation. In the meantime, conversations continue to unfold both in the execution of the task at hand as well as in faculty meetings, private discussions, and lunch table conversations.

Subsequent Actions

Although many staff members remain skeptical that Joan's emphasis on collective autonomy will ever be more than fancy words for talking to each other more often, the level of outward resistance and tension about the task at hand has noticeably subsided. There is no guarantee that research will substantiate the beliefs that the faculty embraces, but even in these instances where they do not, the experience will be one of learning.

After two months of work, the staff members generate a table that confirms the alignment between the key generalizations and the research findings (see Figure 3.5, pp. 82–83). When the completed chart is presented for consideration, staff members respond enthusiastically; the finished product validates that their core beliefs are in alignment with educational research. The staff suggest that the focus group participants be invited back for an afternoon meeting so that they can update them on the progress of the work.

After the meeting with the focus group, the staff members take on the final phase of the task: to articulate a shared vision to describe what the school will look like (visually) when the beliefs are put into practice. Joan divides the staff into small groups to begin to develop these visualizations and provides them with three focusing questions for their work:

1. What does the generalization look like when it is in use?
2. What would I see in a classroom where it was put into practice well (and not so well)?
3. What will teachers *and* students be doing when the generalization has been put into practice? (Adapted from Hall & Hord, 2001, p. 49)

Joan instructs them that each statement is to be "as visual as possible . . . word pictures" (Hall & Hord, 2001, p. 42). The results of their collective endeavor appear in Figure 3.6 (pp. 84–85).

Summing Up and Looking Ahead

By early spring, the teachers in the building are beginning to trust that this innovation requires more than "putting it on paper."

> The school's values and purposes become the driving force. As this happens, a new hierarchy emerges—one that places ideas at the apex and principals, teachers, parents, and students below as members of a shared fellowship that is committed to serving these ideas. (Sergiovanni, 2000, p. 24)

Although staff members remain in an early phase of this process, they solidly stand behind the core beliefs of high achievement and equity and are willing to work together in a new way to make this more of a reality in their building.

Joan's next step: Remembering Henry's earlier comment about the community's call for accountability and the comment made by the local businessman who participated in the focus group ("Don't we need to find out what the data show about how the school currently is honoring these beliefs about achievement and equity? It's really an issue of quality control, not just a wish

3.5

How Best to Achieve Excellence and Equity: Alignment of Beliefs and Findings

Focus Group Beliefs	Excerpts from Research and Theoretical Findings
Students learn best when they can connect all the discrete pieces of knowledge they are learning. It is in the inference making that the learning takes place.	Bransford, Brown, & Cocking (2000) • "Young children actively engage in making sense of their worlds." (p. 234) • "The ability to think and solve problems requires well-organized knowledge that is accessible in appropriate contexts." (p. 153) • "Effective comprehension and thinking requires a coherent understanding of the organizing principles in any subject matter." (p. 238)
Students learn best when they are curious. What engages them is a problem that they see as worth solving, one that is meaningful to them. This experience motivates them to ask questions and to plan strategies for solving the problem.	Bransford, Brown, & Cocking (2000) • "Children are problem solvers, and through curiosity, generate questions and problems. Children attempt to solve problems presented to them, and they also seek novel challenges." (p. 234) • "Learners of all ages are more motivated when they can see the usefulness of what they are learning and when they can use that information to do something that has an impact on others." (p. 261)
Students learn best when the purpose of their learning and the expectations for them are clear. They don't have to guess what they are supposed to learn or how well they are expected to learn it.	Bransford, Brown, & Cocking (2000) • "Students at all levels, but increasingly so as they progress through the grades, focus their learning attention and energies on the parts of the curriculum that are assessed." (p. 245) • "Metacognition refers to people's abilities to predict their performances on various tasks . . . and to monitor their current levels of mastery and understanding (e.g., Brown, 1975; Flavell, 1973)." (p. 12) Marzano (2003) • "Achievement scores in classes where clear learning goals were exhibited were 0.55 standard deviations higher than the achievement scores for classes where clear learning goals were not established." (p. 35, citing research by Mark Lipsey and David Wilson, 1993)

3.5 *(continued)*
How Best to Achieve Excellence and Equity: Alignment of Beliefs and Findings

Focus Group Beliefs	Excerpts from Research and Theoretical Findings
We achieve equity best when we hold all students to the same high-quality standards.	Marzano (2003) • "High expectations of students has been one of the most consistent findings in the literature . . ." that define the characteristics of the most effective schools. (p. 36, quoting David Reynolds and Charles Teddlie, 2000) Williams (1996) • "Latino students succeeded best when 'the teachers assumed that the children were competent and capable and that it was the teacher's responsibility to provide the students with a challenging, innovative, and intellectually rigorous curriculum.'" (p. 58, citing and quoting L. Moll) • To narrow the achievement gap "teachers provide an academically challenging curriculum that includes attention to the development of higher-level cognitive skills." (p. 65)
We achieve equity best when we ensure students have equal access to all learning opportunities.	Marzano (2003) • "Opportunity to learn (OTL) has the strongest relationship with student achievement of all school factors . . . ." (p. 22)

list of who we hope to be"), Joan realizes that data will have to be gathered around student achievement and teacher and student behaviors seen and heard throughout the school. This range of data will have to be collected in order to correctly identify gaps that can serve as the impetus for systemic change. Her challenge is to figure out a way to do this without threatening the staff.

Henry and Ed's next step: They must think through how the work in Joan's school complements and perhaps competes with the district agenda. This not only has to do with the content and process of the envisioning work, but also with the assumptions about who is in control of the system. Although these district-level conversations are not an active part of the story line of this

3.6

Vision of Our School When Our Core Beliefs Are Put into Practice

Focus Group Beliefs	Vision
Students learn best when they can connect all the discrete pieces of knowledge they are learning. It is in the inference making that the learning takes place.	• I will see classroom instruction dominated by questions and explorations, not lecture. • I will see instruction that focuses on discovering the concepts that lie at the heart of each discipline and how the concept is an inference about the relationship among items of knowledge in the discipline. • I will hear students, in class discussion and performance, making connections among discrete pieces of knowledge and/or skill and then regularly revisiting these inferences to check for their continued adequacy. When an inference is found to be inadequate, I will hear students reflect and revise to accommodate new information arising from new learning. • I will see evidence that students do well at tests of knowledge, measures of performance on open-ended prompts, and challenges requiring the use of knowledge and skill in new, important, and authentic ways. • I will see a consistently high level of student achievement across this variety of assessment instruments.
Students learn best when they are curious. What engages them is a problem that they see as worth solving, one that is meaningful to them. This experience motivates them to ask questions and plan strategies for solving the problem.	• I will see curricula and classrooms that are organized around problems. The content of the course becomes the means for solving the problem. • I will see classrooms where students consistently raise the established essential questions that are designed to be the guide for learning. • I will hear students who can explain the importance of the learning they are engaged in and how it will be of future value to them. This explanation is not expressed in platitudes but instead reflects a clear grasp of the transfer value of the learning. • I will see a classroom that emphasizes the development and evaluation of multiple problem-solving strategies, identifying the most promising and being adaptable as the strategies are tested. • I will see students competently use knowledge and skill in new, important ways to solve realistic problems.

3.6 (continued)

Vision of Our School When Our Core Beliefs Are Put into Practice

Focus Group Beliefs	Vision
Students learn best when the purpose of their learning and the expectations for them are clear. They don't have to guess what they are supposed to learn and how well they are expected to learn it.	• I will see a clear rubric for scoring excellence for every product or performance students are asked to generate. • I will see a common set of school rubrics for the same traits in performance used consistently across teachers and subjects. In cases in which rubrics must be discipline specific, the faculty will agree to this modification, and the students will understand the reason for the required modification. • I will see students who can apply the school's rubrics to their own work and to the work of peers and assess at a high level of reliability with the score assigned by the teacher.
We achieve equity best when we hold all students to the same high-quality expectations.	• I will see (a) curriculum that sets high standards for all students, (b) instruction and teacher communication that foster the meeting of these standards, and (c) a rich variety of assessments that provides students the opportunity to demonstrate mastery. • I will see a common set of school rubrics for the same traits in performance used consistently across teachers and subjects. • I will see students internalizing high standards and revising their work to come closer to meeting such standards.
We achieve equity best when we ensure students have equal access to all learning opportunities.	• I will see curriculum that articulates key concepts, content, and skills that are necessary for all students to learn and instruction targeted to ensure all students learn these essentials. • I will see school programs being implemented that prepare all students for learning and success. • I will see all students having equitable access to all educational programs.

book, the operating principles and six steps of continuous improvement continue to serve as relevant guidance for how to approach the conversations.

The reader's next step: With your school and your district in mind, consider the following questions:

➤ What are our core beliefs? Who defined them? Was the group appropriately inclusive?

➤ Where do our beliefs fit within those held by the school district? The state? Is there an appropriate overlap? If not, whose beliefs hold primacy? Who mediates to achieve congruence?

➤ Is our vision abstract or concrete? Would we recognize the vision if we saw it and agree on the recognition?

➤ Is the vision a parochial statement or is it grounded in respected research and theory?

DEFINING REALITY THROUGH DATA

4

Essential Question

What are the gaps between what we believe and what we do? How do we close those gaps?

Operating Principles

– Once staff members commit to the shared vision, they must gain clarity on their responsibility for achieving that vision.

– When staff members perceive data to be valid and reliable in collection and analysis, data both confirm what is working well and reveal the gaps between the current reality and the shared vision in a way that inspires collective action.

Chapter Overview

In a competent system, data are "signposts" on the road to continuous improvement (Schmoker, 1996, p. 30). For the signposts to be trusted as valid and reliable, they must be constructed collaboratively. In other words, data collection and analysis must be grounded in rich conversations about the information as well as how different people make meaning of that information. Although some participants may disagree with some of the particulars about what data are collected, and how that data are analyzed and synthesized, they can all learn to trust that the information will be used to pursue shared goals that will help close the gaps between the vision and the reality.

➤

This chapter takes the reader through the third step of continuous improvement—the collection, analysis, and use of data—and reveals the challenges that teachers and administrators face when they make an honest assessment of teaching and learning practices. "Although schools rarely use data and results to inform practice, data should be an essential feature of how schools do business" (Schmoker, 1996, p. 30). To overcome the fear of what the data will indicate and how the data will be used, staff must collaborate in the collection and analysis so that the resulting information is trusted to be an accurate signpost of current performance.

In this chapter a new character is introduced who will have a real impact on the nature of the work of the school. Ann is a teacher who is highly respected by building and district staff as an "E. F. Hutton": when she talks, people listen. The source of her power is not built into a job description, but rather emanates from her critical perspective on what quality learning is and isn't, as well as her capacity to clearly articulate what others are feeling. She has followed through on her leadership talents in only a handful of ways throughout her 25 years of teaching: serving a couple of terms as a union representative, as a key player in the district's work on supervision and evaluation, and as chairperson of the district committee for the Teacher of the Year award. As far as staff development is concerned, Ann exemplifies the dilemma illustrated in Chapter 1 of a teacher dedicated to continued professional growth but focused largely on the issues that are meaningful to her. If her colleagues are also interested, she collaborates with them, but she doesn't drive anyone's agenda other than her own.

Signposts on the Road to Continuous Improvement

Administrator Conversation #3

Henry: I appreciate your getting back to me so quickly. Did the end result that the faculty came up with measure up to your expectations?

Joan: That's an interesting choice of words. A year ago, I think I would have answered that question based simply on whether they produced what I asked them to and on whether what they produced had value for them. Now, I find myself drawn as much to their emotional response to what they are doing as to the finished product. So, in a much richer way than I would have been able to say before, yes, I am thrilled with where we are right now.

Joan gives Henry and Ed a copy of the "Alignment of Beliefs and Findings" and "Vision of Our School" charts (Figures 3.5 and 3.6) and begins to talk them through the process of how the work was completed.

   Henry: The shared vision is different from what I expected.
   Joan: How so?
   Henry: I expected it to be a sweeping declaration of what we aspire to be. The kind of document that is more inspirational than functional.
   Ed: What's wonderful about the specificity of the goals you fleshed out with the staff is that they seem not only tangible but also assessable.
   Joan: And that's exactly what we're trying to do. We need to be really clear with each other on what it is that we believe and what we'll see when those beliefs are put into practice.
   Ed: The only place where I feel a little lost is . . . what happened to the two core beliefs of high academic achievement and equity? They seem every-where and nowhere in the chart.

Joan goes to a flip chart and sketches a diagram (Figure 4.1) to illustrate where the school has been (the envisioning process carried out in Chapter 3) and where it is headed next (using data to identify gaps and to develop strate-gic plans to close those gaps).

   Henry: *[Looking intently at the diagram]* Although I'm pleased to see where you've placed data on the flowchart, what kind of data collection do you think will yield the information you need? *[Henry points back to one of the vision statements from the "Vision of Our School" chart (Figure 3.6) and reads aloud.]* "I will see classrooms where students consistently raise the established essential questions that are designed to be the guide for learning." There's only one way to get that kind of information—classroom observation.
   Ed: Or teachers reporting in.
   Henry: But how reliable is that information? The validity of that would depend on whether teachers can accurately distinguish between those

students who use questions as a way to construct meaning and those students who use them to repeat back what they've read or heard someone else say. Not sure that this is going to be doable, Joan.

4.1

Conversations Centered on Continuous Improvement in a Competent System

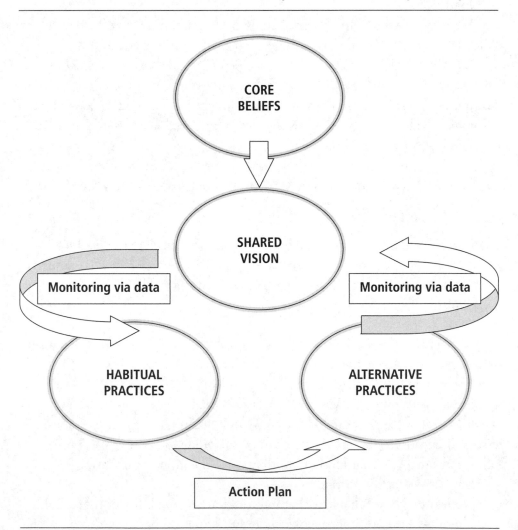

Joan: I totally agree with you that data will need to be collected in ways that are new and different for all of us.

Ed: And for the teachers' union.

Joan: But I think my staff values the shared vision enough that they'll be committed to doing whatever it takes to make it happen.

Henry: Frankly, I think you're being naïve. What they've produced so far is powerful on paper but largely impotent in practice. There's no way that they can be held accountable for change unless there are different data collection mechanisms in place.

Ed: Well, let's put our heads together and figure out what Joan and the staff will need to consider in order to develop a data analysis plan that will be functional and palatable.

Joan: It has got to be more than palatable to my staff. It has got to be accepted by them as the only way to achieve continuous improvement. I don't care if they like the idea or not, if they look forward to doing it or not. I only care that they accept it as part of the reality and integrity of this system.

The three administrators think aloud together for the next 45 minutes to develop a series of concerns and ideas for consideration. To meet Joan's need to help the staff function as active problem solvers in the data analysis process, they refine their work, which results in five key questions (adapted from Glickman, 1993, pp. 48–54):

1. What do we have to find out?
2. What data are currently available?
3. What new data do we need?
4. How do we obtain data?
5. How can we collect data in a valid and reliable form?

Staff Conversation #5

At the next faculty meeting, Joan presents the need for data collection and analysis as the "logical next step" in the envisioning process. "To find out where we already are successful and where we still have room to grow, we must get an accurate picture of reality." She then poses the first four questions she developed with Henry and Ed. Joan divides the faculty into groups, assigning all groups the responsibility for defining the kind of data they will need to determine the degree to which the various parts of the vision are already present in the school. As the groups begin the assigned task, an uncommon quiet settles over the room. Joan is puzzled by the awkward, stunted conversations among the participants. It is so unlike last year when the faculty discussed the chart, setting out the generalizations and research findings. She moves among the groups but fails to identify a general pattern to explain the quiet.

The door to the room opens and a custodian signals to Joan. Joan steps out and the custodian tells her that the gate to the playing field will not lock. Joan, somewhat annoyed, tells the custodian to call district maintenance, tell them of the urgency, and, if need be, chain the gate shut with a padlock. Joan reflects: "Changing my habits is only part of the challenge; I've also got to acclimate staff to changes in their job description if I'm ever going to be able to focus on the real work of the school."

As Joan steps back into the room, she notes a sharp contrast to what was happening when she left. The discussions are now very animated, almost heated. Joan approaches one of the groups. The group falls silent immediately.

Joan: How's it going so far?

Ann: The first vision statement says, "I will see." What does this mean? Miguel said it means we're going to be observed. But who observes? You? Central office? It strikes me as the worst case of "snoopervision," something we tried to get away from when we redid the supervision and evaluation policy a couple of years back.

Miguel: Joan, we really were feeling good about our work when we developed the shared vision statement. It sent a message that you trusted us. Turns out that you were just paving the way for a more intrusive type of top-down management where we are constantly going to be under scrutiny.

Joan reels from the assault. The rest of the groups have become quiet; everyone is listening. It becomes obvious that the content of this conversation has been actively discussed in other groups around the room. As Joan works to regain her composure and focus, she sees Susan stand up and nod at her, indicating a desire to address the concern.

Susan: Maybe it's because I originally worked in the business world, but I don't find this task so scary. In my old job, we always saw data gathering as part of every ongoing project and as part of every new innovation. "Which marketing approach is working best? Is it the one you tried or the one I am using?" We were never judging each other; it was the approach that was being judged. When it came to collecting the data, it was the team that did the collection and analysis. This was our job, not the job of our bosses. We've been working as a team. Why not continue? Let's figure out how we can collect data not on people but on what we see across the school as habitual practices. We've identified what we need to see; is it here?

Ann: But this is not a place of business. This is about more than the bottom line.

Ann's and Susan's comments break the conversation among the staff wide open. Discussion flies fast and furious.

➤ *There are bottom lines here. The state has them for us, and we have them for ourselves.*

➤ *Isn't that why we were so attracted to the envisioning process? Because we actually had the opportunity to articulate what our collective bottom line is?*

➤ *But if the agenda all along was to develop a shared vision and then in a highly intrusive, highly suspect manner collect "data" on what's "really happening" in my room, I never would have supported writing the shared vision in the first place.*

➤ *Observations conducted by outsiders capture only a small piece of a larger picture of what's really happening in the classroom. Even if we have a whole bunch of small pieces, that doesn't mean that we have a sense of the whole picture of what teaching and learning looks like in this school.*

➤ *I want to have a clear vision of what we're working for. To play with the puzzle metaphor, it's using the picture on the box cover as a reference point*

➤

to think about progress and next steps. And I want the opportunity to use that vision to figure out whether I'm on the right track in the work I'm doing with my students. If that makes this a "place of business," then I'm OK with that.

➤ *But who can measure whether or not we're doing this except for teachers? We've got to trust the people who know best to assess whether or not the students are learning.*

➤ *But who sets the benchmarks? Student learning at what levels?*

Joan: *[Resuming control over the direction of the meeting]* We've been working as a team. That has been critical and will continue to be critical to our collective success. This is not about me and not about you; it's about us and our success as a school. I want to pull us back together as a whole group and brainstorm ways to collect the data needed when the vision statement calls for evidence of "seeing" and "hearing." Initially, the one guideline for all comments is that they must ensure that we're looking at the school's practices, not the practice of a single teacher.

In the 40 minutes left for the faculty meeting, the group identifies the following clear guidelines to reflect their real concerns about trust:

1. Develop an observation protocol to identify exactly what information will be gathered.
2. Develop a reporting form to ensure that data are reported in a consistent manner.
   (a) The reports should not identify the teacher of the class observed or the identity of the observer.
   (b) The reports should be placed in a sealed box in the office.
3. Observe every teacher twice, using the protocol and the reporting form.
   (a) Each of the two observations will be conducted by a different staff member.
   (b) All teachers and administrators will conduct observations.

Joan: I think we have a good draft of a plan. We need to spell it out in memo form, then develop the observation protocol and the reporting form.

We also will need to identify who will summarize the data collected. I'm asking Ann and Susan to join me as a writing team to draft these pieces and get them back to you within two weeks.

Susan quickly nods and smiles, acknowledging her willingness. Ann, however, still appears put off by the whole idea. Ann approaches Joan after the meeting adjourns.

Ann: I'm still very uncomfortable, but will agree to help for now because I refuse to see these observations used as a punitive tool.

Joan: You represent a very important perspective.

Ann: What perspective is that? The perspective of being suspicious that this whole observation protocol will turn into an individual witch-hunt? The perspective of not wanting to open up Pandora's box? You've got to be kidding yourself if you think that this protocol is going to pass muster with the union. I see a grievance in your future if you don't sit down and have a lengthy conversation with the union leaders.

Joan: Do you think that we'll be able to find some common ground to collect the data we need to move forward?

Ann: Only if the data *we* need are really trusted to be more than the data *you* want. The tenor of the conversation in the meeting made it clear that staff don't trust this.

Joan: But part of my job is to reeducate them on the value of data. Just because this hasn't been done before doesn't mean it isn't worth doing. This is not data on individual staff members; this is data on the school. How many more times do I need to say this?

Ann: As many times as it takes until we believe you. That hasn't happened yet. Better to acknowledge this point and work from it than to bury your head in the sand. If you don't take care of it now, it will take care of you later.

Principal Reflection #5

That evening, Joan can't shake the meeting from her thoughts. She realizes that Henry's comment about her naïveté is more on target than she

➤

wanted to admit at the time. She also knows that the success of the effort will depend on her success in the role of leader-facilitator. That seems overwhelming. How can she possibly anticipate the myriad needs of all the individuals on the staff? How can she cultivate the trust that is so clearly lacking among the staff? It amazes her that they could have even written a shared vision statement when such suspicion still exists between teacher and administrator. She assumed that trust had been built, and is unhappy and uncomfortable to discover that she was wrong. Is she better off knowing this? Absolutely. But it sure doesn't feel that way tonight.

Analysis of Staff Conversation #5 and Principal Reflection #5

The issue of trust appears again (and will reappear again and again). Joan continues to be blindsided by an issue that clearly other staff members have oriented her to already: Henry called her naïve, Rob mocked the "collaboration" among staff, and Maria emphasized that people tend to say one thing and then do another. The uncomfortable realization that Joan makes here is if she doesn't deepen trust among staff it will mean the termination of the continuous improvement effort. This is reminiscent of one of the operating principles discussed at length in Chapter 2: *Every staff member must be regarded as a trusted colleague in the examination of habitual practices.* Trust can exist, but it is the deepening of that trust that is the necessary and ongoing job of leaders.

Staff Conversation #6

Thanks to the work of Ann and Susan, Joan is able to get the protocol and reporting form out to staff along with a schedule of observations. Joan has met with the union leaders to review the observation protocol and the plan for data analysis. They negotiate steps that ensure the anonymity of the observation reports and the final data. They also agree that all staff members will be released from their assigned duties for two periods to conduct the observations.

As contentious as the planning of the data collection has been, there is surprisingly little grumbling when the staff receives the protocol and it comes time to carry out the observations. Staff members seem to trust the purpose for the observations that the protocol has called for and that the data will be used as a learning opportunity (as opposed to a police action).

After the time needed to train the entire staff in the use of the reporting form and to complete the two rounds of observations, Joan calls a meeting with Susan and Ann. They analyze the data, and find the following:

> ➤ Seventy percent of the instructional time was used for teacher delivery of information to students.
> ➤ Eighteen percent of the instructional time was taken by teacher questions.
>   – Seventy-eight percent of the time the questions were seeking specific pieces of information.
>   – Twenty-two percent of the time the questions were asking the students to explore connections among facts and develop tentative conclusions (inferences).
> ➤ Twelve percent of the instructional time was spent on other activities.
> ➤ One hundred percent of teachers use some form of rubric to score student work, but only the language arts teachers use the same rubrics, and then only for writing. Three teachers also use the writing rubric when scoring social studies essays.
> ➤ Seventy-five percent of the students were meeting goal on the state-mandated standardized tests.
> ➤ Fifteen percent of teachers have developed units that articulate how student work is designed to be in alignment with state content standards.
> ➤ Ninety-seven percent of the students had a 3.0 grade average or better on their report cards.
> ➤ Eighty percent of the assessments were traditional tests of discrete knowledge; fifteen percent were open-ended academic prompts; five percent were authentic performance tasks.

Over the course of the next several late afternoons, the data slowly come together in categories but without explicit meaning. Both Ann and Susan raise the issue of what the next step is. Susan suggests that the three of them draw up some conclusions to accompany a report to the faculty. Ann is ada-mantly opposed.

Ann: Although the three of us compiled the data, determining what it means is a job the full staff should address.

Joan: I completely agree. We have our last staff development half-day next week. We'll present the data and collectively analyze the findings.

Ann: Are the data going to be shared outside the school?

Joan: Although we need to share the information with Ed and Henry because we are part of the district, it will be up to us to draw conclusions about what the data actually say and how we can use the data to do an even better job. It will be *our* report, *our* analysis, and *our* honesty. It's too early to share with the wider community. That will come, but only when we have a plan for closing any gaps. We'll be honest and proactive.

Ann: I hope we won't be sorry when we share this information with the rest of the school community.

Analysis of Staff Conversation #6

Why has this series of conversations been so hard? Why the disconnect between data and achievement of goals? Because of a lack of trust. This is typical in an incompetent system in which educators ignore the link between evidence of achievement and the way things are done. This is what Schmoker (1996) describes as a "tacit bargain among constituents at every level not to gather or use information that will reveal where we need to do better, where we need to make changes" (p. 33). Although the staff members appreciate the need for monitoring via data on a cognitive level, on an emotional level many resent how data intrude upon their individual autonomy.

> ➤ *Data are scary.*
> ➤ *Data are my enemy. Data point out what is wrong with what I'm doing and emphasize how I don't measure up.*
> ➤ *The very fact that people are collecting data shows that they don't trust that I am doing a good job.*

From this narrow vantage point, data are almost certain to tear people apart instead of bringing them together. The tension and distrust that have emerged in the conversations reinforce the fact that the staff members in this system do not think systemically; they approach data through the personal domain of their students and their professionalism.

Three primary concerns feed this resentment. First, data analysis unlocks the door to what has previously been a relatively private domain: the quality of student work within an individual classroom. Teachers are trusted to keep private grade books, to develop their own assessment vehicles, scoring mechanisms, and objectivity standards; they are the judges of success and failure on hundreds of assignments for dozens of students throughout the year. The notion that their assessment and evaluation system could be analyzed by someone who does not know their students personally seems instantly offensive to many educators; they believe that they know their students better and therefore have more valid insights into how to improve student performance. Data analysis, however, provides a powerful opportunity to work collaboratively with others to identify common strengths and weaknesses and to identify systemic solutions. This logic seems "backward" at first glance: to gain more insight into your own students, engage in an analysis with other teachers about their students. For this analysis to be successful, teachers must be evaluating students on common measures and must believe that the system performs better as a result of the collective endeavors.

Second, data analysis will inevitably result in a mandate for change. "Data almost always point to action—they are the enemy of comfortable routines" (Schmoker, 1996, p. 33). Although educators are accustomed to change, in an incompetent system they endure "dog-and-pony shows" because they know that the innovation will move in and out of the building within a short period of time with minimal expectations of implementation. In a competent system, however, in which data signal gaps between current practice and desired results, change becomes difficult to avoid. On an individual level, people become conscious that what they are doing doesn't match their personal beliefs. On a systems level, people become conscious that what they are being asked to do will be evaluated in classrooms across the building to judge the approach's effectiveness.

Third, data analysis is public information and will likely spawn increased pressure for accountability if results are poor. The implication is that student performance could be linked (either reasonably or not) to teacher performance. This causality between the quality of teaching and student achievement highlights educators' fear about their ability (and the school's ability) to raise performance levels. Despite the tendency to avoid or mistrust those who call for results, teachers will find that data and results can be powerful forces for generating an intrinsic desire to improve. Properly done, "accountability and improvement can be effectively interwoven, but it requires great sophistication" (Fullan & Stiegelbauer, 1991, p. 87). Joan and her staff have laid the foundation for this type of improvement effort because of their work creating a shared vision with the input of key stakeholders in the school community. Schmoker (1996) validates the power of this type of approach: "A concern with results and improvement can satisfy and energize every constituent, from the practitioner, to the parent, to the school board" (p. 36). Teachers are no longer isolated in their efforts to move students toward the shared vision; all members of the community are informed participants in the effort (which is why vision statements are written in such concrete terms).

It also is necessary to underscore the importance of language and tone in effective data analysis. Regardless of personal style or agenda, the data report should be motivated by "systems modeling": a disciplined examination of reality that has relevance and meaning for all staff, at all grades, at all levels, in all jobs.

> Systems modeling imposes a discipline for clarity and consistency that ordinary language, either spoken or written, does not require. In ordinary conversation, people often hide behind ambiguous, incomplete, and even illogical statements, such as: "The way people respond depends on the situation." A systems modeler would have to specify: *which* people, *what* kinds of responses, and exactly *how* different conditions would lead to particular actions. (Senge et al., 2000, p. 235)

One of the most effective ways to ensure clear language, a collaborative process, and valid priorities is to have staff members produce data summaries. According to McTighe and Thomas (2003), data summaries are invaluable because they enable staff to do the following:

1. Describe current student achievement in a concrete and comprehensive way that directs action.
2. Identify priorities that are likely to emerge for which measurable goals can then be developed.
3. Present a synthesis of the evidence rather than attributing blame.
4. Foster ownership of performance data. (Adapted from pp. 52–55)

Subsequent Actions and Resulting Staff Conversation

All the staff members receive the raw data before the weekend, and Joan asks them to use their next scheduled team meetings to identify any patterns. A full faculty meeting takes place after the team meetings. At the faculty meeting, Joan divides the staff into groups. She directs participants to spend the next 45 minutes developing inferences about the degree to which the school is achieving its vision. These inferences arise from patterns suggested by the data. Once these are reported out, recorded, and displayed, the group turns to any data that have not yet been included and incorporates the data into the inferences. At the end of the meeting, the faculty feels confident that the two lists they have created—one indicating gaps between vision and reality and the other indicating areas where there are no gaps—contain obvious information. For instance, all of the teachers use rubrics, but the only rubrics that have been developed and implemented in common are in language arts.

Joan closes the meeting by commending the staff on its insights. She also comments on the important role that disagreements have played in the small- and large-group discussions. By addressing the disagreements openly, the faculty's thinking has been sharpened. She then sets up the next step.

Joan: Now comes the important work of planning what we do next with the conclusions. What plans do we make to close gaps? How do we ensure that any plans do not threaten the areas where gaps do not exist?

After the meeting has concluded, Ann approaches Joan, who is already listening to Susan's feedback on the meeting.

Ann: I think that went surprisingly well. I do feel as if we know what the school looks like. It's not an assessment of individuals; it's a picture of the whole. I thank you, Susan, for the redirection. I thank you, Joan, for the trust in us. But I do want to state the importance of constant vigilance by all of us.

Several days later, Joan's secretary tells her that Ann and two other teachers want to know if Joan could schedule them in today for an appointment. Two hours later, all three teachers gather in Joan's office for a conversation.

Ann: Joan, the three of us have been talking about the conclusions we drew at our meeting last week. One of the big ideas was that our students aren't clear enough on the purpose of a class or the key concepts and skills that we want them to get. We also said we need more consistency across the board, especially in how we evaluate student work. In addition, we said that instruction revolved more around lecture than on inference building and refining. This all seemed daunting to us when we left, but over lunch the three of us were talking about how all these themes were addressed before. Remember, because of Henry's new agenda on developing a standards-based curriculum, he paid for the three of us to attend an intensive workshop last summer? At the time, we knew that the methods set out in the workshop were very complex; we couldn't handle them individually without a lot of support. Although you agreed that we needed to spend some time talking through the experience and the vision for the work in this school, we never really got around to having the conversation. We think that this might be a good time to have the conversation, given our current commitment to closing the gaps. This innovation has the potential to help us get clearer on what we expect all kids to know, be able to do, and understand. It also provides direction on how to measure the students' achievement of these things.

The four of them then discuss the idea that all planning has to be driven by a clear definition of the understandings that a teacher wants students to achieve. This is clearly related to the shared vision's focus on high academic achievement. The emphasis on curriculum and assessment design instead of delivery seems to be the right fit. Joan asks the teachers to share their information and ideas with their colleagues before the next faculty meeting. They agree.

At the faculty meeting, there is a general consensus that they are on the right track, but the staff members are very honest about the fact that they have no idea how that concept would play itself out in practice.

It is late May already, and the time for planning next year's staff development is growing short. On the one hand, a direction needs to be established for the work. On the other hand, for the direction to bring the system closer to its vision, staff will have to be clear on how any approach will facilitate that process.

Sarah (a member of Anne's grade-level team): What's the name of the program that you heard about at the workshop you went to, Ann? I remember you telling me about it last year when you came home.

Ann: It's not a program; it's an approach called *Understanding by Design*.

Sarah: Let's not worry about semantics. Does it have potential?

Ann: Yes, but it *is* a question of semantics because I don't want anyone in the room to believe that this innovation prescribes what we want students to understand. That is the domain, as it should be, of this staff.

Joan: And the department of education, and the district, and established thought in the various subject areas.

Sarah: *[Chuckling]* I hear you, I hear you. Just tell us what to do next. How are we going to learn about this approach so we can decide if the fit is there?

After more discussion, Joan and the staff outline a multitiered approach to get staff the information they need so they can evaluate the relevance of the innovation to achieving the shared vision.

➤ Joan will attend a week-long workshop on *Understanding by Design* being held in July and will pay for several teachers who are interested in the training experience to join her.

➤ Joan will purchase 10 copies of the book *Understanding by Design* (Wiggins & McTighe, 1998) so interested staff can do some background reading over the summer.

➤ Joan will hire a consultant for the first staff development day in August to provide an overview of the innovation for the full staff so that they will all have at least a rudimentary knowledge of what *Understanding by Design* is and isn't. They will then have a conversation on the following staff development day to explore together the viability of the innovation.

Summing Up and Looking Ahead

In a competent system, data collection and analysis function as a formative rather than a summative assessment, both in principle and in practice. The first hurdle is to talk through the intent of the data collection process in order to debunk the myth that numbers will lead to individual witch-hunts (instead of collective accountability) and a diluted curriculum that minimizes teacher creativity and mandates teaching to the test (instead of an enriched curriculum that raises student achievement for all). Once staff members are open to the possibility that data can produce an accurate picture of the current system's performance, they come to appreciate that this evidence is more reliable and informative than a collection of teacher anecdotes. It transcends individual classrooms, personalities, and circumstances. Another reason that the staff members adapt to this "new way of doing business" is that the data collection and analysis are performed in service to the shared vision (as opposed to an administrator's or policymaker's individual agenda). The data inform the staff about the gaps between the shared vision and the current reality so they can produce a collective mandate for change that is in alignment with their core beliefs. Because the mandate emerges from this collective analysis and because it addresses areas of concern that have been identified and quantified in the system, participants will be much more invested in the staff development plan.

Joan's next step: She will attend the summer workshop on *Understanding by Design* and find a consultant who is both knowledgeable in the content, capable of systemic thinking, and accessible to her staff.

The teachers' next step: They will decide what amount of information they want to acquire about *Understanding by Design* before the start of the next school year. They can attend the summer workshop with Joan, borrow existing resources on the subject, or wait until the August staff development day.

Regardless of their individual decisions, they are clear that they have a responsibility to evaluate whether this innovation will help put their shared vision into operation.

The reader's next step: With your school and your district in mind, consider the following questions.

➤ Is our vision assessable? What are the gaps between our vision and reality?

➤ What existing structures are in place to evaluate the effectiveness of curriculum, assessment, and instruction? What data do they generate? Is it enough?

➤ What data are needed if the success of the school's system is to be validly and reliably determined? Are the data direct or indirect? Are they credible? Is there a standard for credibility?

➤ Who "owns" the data? Who should? Why?

➤ Is data collection seen as being a measure of individual competence? Program competence? School competence? School district competence?

➤ Are there issues of trust that get in our way? What are they? Where are they? Where is trust strongest? Why? Are there experiences here that can be used to address a lack of trust in other areas? What are these experiences? How can they be used?

5 Designing and Implementing Staff Development That Matters

Essential Questions

What are our priorities? How are they connected?

Operating Principles

– All staff must see the content and process of staff development as a necessary means to achieve the desired end.

– It is not the number of innovations addressed in the staff development plan but rather the purposeful linkage among them that makes systemic change possible and manageable.

Chapter Overview

This chapter focuses on step four of the continuous improvement plan: identifying the innovations that will most likely close the gaps between the vision and the current reality. Up to this point, staff could participate in the conversations and decisions in isolation from their habitual practices. Now that the data are in, the school has a concrete, information-driven picture of current performance levels, which means that what staff "do" in the classroom becomes a subject of open examination.

Four key challenges are explored in this chapter. First, the staff must achieve consensus on which innovations will be addressed immediately and over the long term to raise student achievement. Second, these innovations must be "bundled" so that staff members believe they are working on a unified plan instead of a number of competing changes. Third, the collective work of the school has to function within the context of the larger K–12 system. Fourth, Joan must broaden the leadership of the change effort to ensure that the work is "humanely oriented" by creating a change facilitator team that consistently assesses where teachers are, what they need to move forward, and how to allocate resources to meet those needs (Hall & Hord, 2001, p. 28).

Laying the Groundwork for Implementation

Staff Conversation #7

The auditorium seat initially resists and then emits a long, piercing screech when Susan pushes it down to sit. "Sorry about the noise! Guess they never got around to giving these chairs a tune-up last year," she says to Maria and Rob, who are seated next to her. Before the principal kicks off the beginning of the year's staff development program, the three teachers still have time for a few moments of conversation. Susan asks, "Prepared to be a continuous improver today, Rob?" Rob flashes a smile back and holds up a large cup of coffee. "How about you, Maria?" Maria waves the school vision statement that they developed last year, honoring a request from the principal that everyone bring a copy today. It is good to see Rob and Maria again. Susan has missed thinking aloud together. Although some of their meetings last year ran a little long, she believes that those conversations and the ensuing work with staff members have brought a new level of seriousness and direction to the building.

Joan walks to the lectern and welcomes the staff to "what is sure to be an exciting opportunity for us all." The audience offers some polite applause as Joan launches into her opening speech.

Today is our day. It's the first day of many more days to come full of collegial conversations about what all students are expected to know and be able to do and how we make that happen in a powerful, positive, universal way for every student. I'm not preaching to you from a mountaintop; I'm going to be working next to you in the classrooms and the conference rooms. There are no spectators on this staff; we will change together. Even though this is a team effort, I am keenly aware that the change process begins in a very personal way. We will have opportunities to learn about what any innovation will require us to know and be able to do and to gain clarity about how what we are learning will affect each classroom; and you will have the time, support, and feedback you need as the innovation moves into your classroom. We will not all move at the same pace, but we will all move. I am determined to bring us closer to who we said we wanted to be, and I know that this system cannot change until each member has changed.

Today's presenter asks each of us to think about how we determine goals for student learning, how assessments are designed to measure whether students have achieved those goals, and how students are given the opportunity to work on those goals through a learning plan. The job is not to start filling in boxes of a template; the job is to consider how this backwards-design philosophy can bring each of us, all of us, closer to our vision of a school that values excellence and equity for all.

After sharing the credentials of the consultant and explaining why this consultant's style and approach is the best fit for the staff, Joan slips into the seat next to Maria in the front row. "One of the perks of being principal," she whispers to Maria. "We always get a good seat."

Analysis of Staff Conversation #7

What a difference a year has made. The "déjà vu" built into the opening narrative prompts reflection about what has changed since the last time Joan launched a staff development innovation.

➤ Teachers not only feel collegiality with one another but also feel bonded by their collective efforts to improve performance.
➤ The principal articulates and models that staff development is part of their collective work; she belongs in the front row, not only as an ardent supporter of the work but also as a learner.
➤ Although this work will be collegial, it also is mandated. But this is a collective mandate that serves the shared vision statement.
➤ The "expert" is selected not only for his expertise in the innovation but also because his style fits the uniqueness of this school.
➤ The agenda and expectations for the workshop are clear even before the meeting begins. This workshop was designed in response to a

direct need expressed by the staff to learn more before they discuss implementation of a major staff development innovation. Those staff members who wanted more information before this workshop took advantage of several opportunities offered in the summer.

Despite all of the positive work that has been done, it is likely that some staff members still believe that they can emerge from this journey unchanged (or unscathed); that after the "dog-and-pony show" is over, this new innovation will soon become a distant memory. Hall and Hord (2001) explain: "Such judgments continue to contribute to the decades-old practice of rejecting changes before they've been implemented, leading to the next swing of the pendulum and a new wave of innovations" (p. 28). Joan's leadership in the design phase of the staff development plan is absolutely critical to the continuous improvement effort. She must sustain and expand the collective autonomy that has been built so far to enhance her staff members' confidence that they can do the work, and she must put support structures in place that will help every staff member grow.

Staff Conversation #8

The day after the presentation, Joan has allocated two hours of the afternoon time she has with her staff to discuss next steps. She opens the meeting with a pointed question: "Does *Understanding by Design* have the potential to take us where we need to go?"

Teacher responses highlight some of the components of the approach:

➤ *Sounded like good practice to me, organized in boxes to make sure you don't forget the important stuff.*
➤ *Not a revolutionary way of thinking about teaching and learning. I feel that I'm doing a lot of these things already but that my distinctions aren't as sharp as they could be.*
➤ *Trying to use the "right" terminology, the Understanding by Design terminology, was getting in the way of being able to play with the ideas. How can we really define the understandings if we're too preoccupied with how to say it?*

➤ *The whole day gave me a headache. I've already planned out the first unit, which I'll be introducing to kids in two days, and the workshop really blew apart what I had thought was good work. Now I feel that I have to go back to the drawing board but haven't been taught how to draw by using this technique yet.*

➤ *I see how it can work in our individual classrooms, but I don't see how it can help us systemically. Don't we need to go back to the drawing board together? The unit design template narrowly focuses on our individual work, not on our collective responsibility to improve student results.*

Ann: From the summer academy that a few of us attended last month, we learned how this can be used as a way to think systemically via curriculum mapping, for example. *[There are audible groans around the room.]* I know, I know. That wasn't even last year's innovation; that was at least three or four innovations back, sometime after we were Hunter-ized and before we were "tuned" by some protocols. But seriously, we could use this to redo our curriculum maps.

Maria: I'm not even sure if that sounds nice in theory. We did that once, and all it did was waste time and paper. I thought we were going to get the opportunity to work on designing curriculum units using a backwards-design template. Why are you overcomplicating the situation?

Ann: Because *Understanding by Design* isn't something you do; it's an approach, a way of thinking. It has to be bundled with other innovations or structures, like a curriculum map or a unit.

Miguel: Can't we just play with pieces of the template in isolation first? We could work with essential questions this year and then move on to another piece next year.

Joan: Essential questions are how you engage and focus students in the learning. That means that the desired results must be articulated in order for the questions to have traction in the classroom. We have to know the understandings, the knowledge, and the skills that are the substance of our curriculum.

Susan: It seems that we have two possible options. One, work through a unit design framework; or two, work through a curriculum map framework. What was so awful the first time the maps were completed?

Ann: *[She gestures toward the marker board in the room.]* May I, Joan?
Joan: Absolutely.

After Ann quickly outlines the original framework (Figure 5.1), Miguel jumps back into the conversation and begins to attack the process as a colossal waste of time and effort.

Joan: I appreciate that you have a lot of concerns about the framework, Miguel. But since so many people here completed the original curriculum maps, let's give everyone time to collectively diagnose the strengths and concerns of curriculum mapping based on our experiences from several years ago.

The staff members immediately divide into small groups, as has become standard operating procedure for their collective conversations. Thirty minutes later, the full group reconvenes to report out the content of the small-group conversations. Joan uses the marker board to record staff comments in two

5.1
Original Curriculum Map Template

Subject: _____   Unit Focus: _____   Grade Level:_____

Time of Year	Topics/Content	Concepts	Skills	Major Assessments

Source: Adapted from work completed in Nanuet Public Schools, Nanuet, NY.

columns—one highlighting the strengths of curriculum mapping and the other highlighting the staff's concerns (Figure 5.2).

As the faculty members discuss both the insights they generated and the original process they went through, more and more teachers voice their support for the potential of curriculum maps. Joan listens intently, taking notes on key points. She then summarizes for them the four common themes that ran throughout many of the comments:

> Curriculum mapping can build continuity and consistency for multiple teachers teaching the same course.

> Curriculum mapping can unify curriculum so that all students move smoothly from one level of learning to the next.

> Curriculum mapping can create alignment with the state content standards and ensure that we are helping students meet rigorous expectations in every unit that we teach, while it also honors our own vision of quality curriculum and instruction.

> Curriculum mapping can guide instruction but also can allow individual flexibility and creativity as vital parts of the unit design process.

Rob: So, it seems this approach has a lot of potential for us.

Miguel: Wait a minute! What happened to the long list of concerns about the process? Joan, you've only synthesized the side of the chart that supports what you want us to say. If you expect us to buy into this approach, you have to deal with the fact that there are more concerns than strengths. Doesn't that send an important message?

Ann: [*With a slight smirk on her face because she knows what she is about to say is so like what teachers say to students*] But it's quality, not quantity, that counts. Do the common threads of the strengths outweigh the common threads of the concerns?

Miguel: But how can we move on without at least dignifying the other half? Frankly, if you want us to trust that our contributions matter, actions speak louder than words.

Joan: Fair enough, Miguel.

The staff then analyzes the concerns the same way that the strengths were analyzed. What Miguel and the rest of the staff discover is that Joan's

5.2

Feedback from Teachers on Curriculum Mapping

Strengths of Curriculum Mapping	Concerns Based on Previous Experience
• Organization • Guide for new teachers • Checklist to make sure you covered everything you are supposed to • Represents conversations among designers (logic, sequence of the practitioners who teach the subject) • Allows you to find gaps between grade levels and between local curriculum and state standards • Congruence (all teachers know skills and content focus) between your own grade level and across grade levels—keeps teachers on the "same page" • Accountable to students to honor what you need to "cover" so they are prepared • Makes you feel good about the quality work represented on the map (trust in the document) • Forces communication between parents and children about what they are doing in school (prompts, talking points) • Flexibility—a map "forces you to be free" because it establishes the desired results so that teachers can focus design time on how to most effectively teach students so that they can achieve those results • Helps you to do a better job (by your students, colleagues, administrators, and parents) • Big picture is there—serves as a framework or foundation to organize the course/grade level • Time frame to budget time • Designates skills and concepts that should be taught to ensure alignment w/state and local standards • Lets you see links between subject areas • Interesting to look at range of assessments	• Time needed to make them • Constricting—time, limiting teacher creativity, different skill levels (assumptions made), different teaching styles • Parents who co-opt the map by teaching ahead of schedule • Calendar lock-in doesn't work as a generalization—time schedules are more personalized than that • Sense of ownership is different if you are handed it vs. if you build it • Huge task to undertake • Teachers are making changes to their private curriculum maps, but changes aren't generally reflected in official version • Lack of faith in the integrity/accuracy of the maps • Not user-friendly • Too much information can be overwhelming; too little is not useful • Inconsistencies from map to map • Teachers not really using each other's maps • Potential misuse of the map—not designed to be unfairly used as an accountability mechanism in a narrow-minded, "gotcha" way—doesn't honor reality of ongoing changes • Must have help—can't be a piecemeal process done by a few people • Losing creativity/individuality—can't be too overloaded (promotes only coverage mentality) or too "time bound" • Not always correct (mistakes in topics identified, time frame, out of alignment, not really content standards, missing pieces, assessments needed to follow up, holes) • Building consensus among teachers vs. protecting teacher autonomy? • Adoption of new text materials/resources invalidating a curriculum map • Effort needed to keep the map current

Source: Adapted from work completed in Nanuet Public Schools, Nanuet, NY.

deliberate word choice in the first list (e.g., "can build," "can unify") acknowledges that the strengths are possible only when people are mindful of the serious reservations raised on the other part of the list. Joan asks the teachers if they have any more issues before moving on to the next step.

Susan: I'm actually not so sure if I buy into this yet. This sounds like a great answer to the question, What are we going to do for our staff development work this year? That's very different from what I thought was the question on the table: How will doing this work help close the gaps between where the data say we are and our vision of where we want to be?

Rob: How can you not see the link between the vision statement and this approach? It couldn't be more obvious!

Ann: It could very well be a time-consuming exercise, just like it was last time, that sparks interesting conversations that are never resolved, never finished. Did you notice *[gesturing to her colleagues]* that the conversations we had about the maps were much richer than the maps themselves?

Joan: Why was that?

Ann: Because we became more concerned about having the maps completed within a certain time frame than about their quality.

Maria: Although I agree that we were pushed too far too fast last time, I also think we didn't understand why we were doing what we were doing. It felt much more like a cursory exercise than a serious analysis of teaching and learning.

Ann: We also had no idea what a good curriculum map was supposed to look like. I know our group spent a lot of time trying to figure out if this was a device to audit what we were currently doing or a pedagogical device to think through what we were supposed to be doing.

Susan: And what did you conclude?

Ann: Even though it was interesting to think about the scope and sequence of the curriculum across grade levels, the limited time we had to complete the task pushed these conversations outside the scope of our job. We resigned ourselves to using the maps to record habitual practices and then, after we turned them in, returned to our interesting conversations about serious gaps and repetitions in the curriculum.

Rob: Now I remember. We were given a series of blank boxes, asked to fill them in, and then were told our coordinator would put the documents together. So I guess we did the same thing as Ann's group but without the interesting conversation.

Joan: For those maps to become a useful starting point, they should have been the launching pad for the kinds of conversations that Ann's group had informally.

Susan: But even if those conversations happen formally this time, how will the process of creating, implementing, and communicating these maps help us get closer to the vision statement? What will our school look like once these maps are in place? We're talking about a serious undertaking here—at least two years to get this done. Bottom line: we have to prove to ourselves that it's worth the time.

Joan: Fair enough. We did that work with data last spring to show the gaps between what *is* and what *should be* for a reason. The last thing I want to do now is to push curriculum mapping and *Understanding by Design* on you without real clarity on why we are doing this.

Rob: It seems to me that curriculum mapping will promote both academic achievement and increased equity for all students if all courses are strongly linked to the state content standards. If we're committed to looking closely at the degree of alignment that currently exists between the delivered curriculum and the state standards, I think we'll discover that the right hand doesn't know what the left hand is doing.

Ann: What do you mean?

Rob: I mean that in all of our individual noble intentions to do right by our students, there likely are some serious gaps between what the state holds us accountable to teach kids and what we hold ourselves accountable to teach; and there are some serious gaps and overlaps between what I cover with kids and what the teacher who has the same kids next year covers with them.

Ann: That's exactly why I was excited about *Understanding by Design* in the first place. If we identify the desired results and plan backward, we can then analyze the actual results both vertically and horizontally.

Maria: But I thought that it only worked as a lens to create individual curriculum units, not curriculum maps.

Ann: Isn't curriculum mapping the same idea, just on a larger scale? [*Nods of agreement from much of the audience*] So why don't we try to come up with a curriculum mapping process that will make the interesting conversations vital to the completion of the maps this time?

Susan: Whatever the proposed format will be, the next step has got to be to create a clear picture of what the school will look like once the maps are completed and implemented. Otherwise, it will likely lead to longer interesting conversations with little or no change in how or what we teach.

Joan: First things first. A group of us will get together sometime in the next two weeks to discuss the links among curriculum mapping, *Understanding by Design*, and closing the gaps. We'll then develop a tentative curriculum map template based on our analysis. [*Joan wraps up the meeting by soliciting volunteers for the group analysis on linkage and then dismisses the group.*] Have a wonderful first day with the kids on Monday!

Maria: Oh, that? You mean we have other things to think about besides this? [*Laughter*]

Analysis of Staff Conversation #8

Carl Glickman (1993) has said, "It would be heavenly if school renewal were as easy as the textbooks, illustrations, and diagrams suggest. Fortunately, the process does not lend itself to prescriptions that override the individual context of the school" (p. 144). A staff development innovation cannot simply be replicated based on another school's success or the steps outlined in a manual. The design of the innovation must be personalized to honor the unique complexity and purposefulness of each particular system. Sarason (2002) discusses why "cloning" school reform efforts is untenable:

> To talk about cloning an educational reform is to reinforce the imagery of an impersonal engineering process. It ludicrously oversimplifies what is involved in an effort to spread reform. It mammothly obscures the fact that any noncosmetic reform in one site will inevitably engender resistance when applied to another site. (p. 141)

This is reminiscent of the conversation in Chapter 2 around the operating principle, *"Each school is a complex living system with purpose."* Hall and Hord (2001) highlight two key dimensions that influence the change process:

1. The *physical features,* such as the size and arrangement of the facility, and the resources, policies, structures, and schedules that shape the staff's work
2. The *people factors,* which include the attitudes, beliefs, and values . . . as well as the relationships and norms that guide the individuals' behavior (p. 15)

In addition to tailoring the innovation to make sure that it is in alignment with the physical features and the people factors, we propose a third dimension:

3. The *innovation's potential*—the likelihood that the change will help close the gaps identified between the shared vision and the data-driven reality of current performance levels.

Success or failure of the staff development innovation will largely depend on whether the desired results are possible and whether they are worth the effort. Change will require staff to "unlearn" existing practices, struggle with the uncertainty and frustration about "getting it right," and monitor, adjust, and refine performance to achieve the greatest effect.

Another layer of complexity is that the potential of one innovation leads to exciting (but scary) conversations about all of the other innovations that really "need" to happen at the same time—for example, the unanticipated revelation that staff should pursue *Understanding by Design* and curriculum mapping simultaneously. Joan and her staff must narrow the focus of school improvement to a small handful of tightly linked areas. Fullan (2001) explains the danger of overloading staff with competing efforts at the same time:

> In schools the main problem is not the absence of innovations but the presence of too many disconnected, episodic, piecemeal, superficially adorned projects . . . . The result, according to one associate superintendent, is that "frustration and

anger have never been higher." When attempting to garner new funds or develop new programs, over and over again, he hears from principals and teachers "we don't want anything else. We're over our heads." (pp. 109–110)

In a competent system, instead of being seen as part of an unmanageable number of different changes, innovations are seen as part of a single whole; the more closely linked the innovations are, the easier it is for staff to handle the increased magnitude of change. "[C]hange initiatives are not typically centered around a single innovation but rather a bundle of innovations" (Hall & Hord, 2001, p. 8). No matter how tight the alignment among various change innovations, bundling does require more resources for implementation—resources in time, training, and support. It also adds a layer of complexity to the feedback process, making it even more important to have a common picture of what these changes look like both individually and collectively. The goal, then, is to bundle a handful of innovations and implement them simultaneously rather than sequentially. Joyce and Showers (2002) use the following example to illustrate this approach:

> A school identifies its primary goal as improving the level of student literacy, but secondary goals identify a need for increased faculty cooperation in developing curriculum. The content selected for the staff development program will center on literacy, but the design of training will incorporate peer-coaching teams such that teachers regularly collaborate to develop their literacy curriculum even as they integrate new learning about the teaching of literacy. (p. 65)

Although the linkage between *Understanding by Design* and curriculum mapping appears straightforward to the teachers in the conversation, it is important to review the basic principles behind both innovations to illustrate the connections.

Understanding by Design promotes a backward-design approach to the development or refinement of curriculum, assessment, and instruction. First, designers identify the desired results (Stage 1); then they design assessments (Stage 2) that can measure whether students have met those results. They then create the learning plan (Stage 3) to ensure that students have the opportunity to explore, refine, and articulate what they learn, and become competent at the desired results—a competence revealed by success at the challenge provided by the assessments. (See Figure 5.3.)

The primary goal of *Understanding by Design* is to "engage students in exploring and deepening their understanding of important ideas and the design of assessments to reveal the extent of their understandings" (Wiggins & McTighe, 1998, p. 3). Jay McTighe (2003) documents the connection between this emphasis on inquiry, "uncoverage," and performance assessments, and increased student achievement. "The principles and the practices of [*Understanding by Design*] reflect contemporary views of learning based on research in cognitive psychology and are validated by specific studies of factors influencing student achievement." He then highlights key findings from *How People Learn* (Bransford, Brown, & Cocking, 2000) relevant to *Understanding by Design:*

> ➤ Learning must be guided by generalized principles in order to be widely applicable. Knowledge learned at the level of rote memory rarely transfers; transfer most likely occurs when the learner knows and understands underlying concepts and principles that can be applied to problems in new contexts. Learning with understanding is more likely to promote transfer than simply memorizing information from a text or a lecture.

> ➤ Experts first seek to develop an understanding of problems, and this often involves thinking in terms of core concepts or big ideas. Novices' knowledge is much less likely to be organized around big ideas; they are more likely to approach problems by searching for correct formulas and pat answers that fit their everyday intuitions.

> ➤ Research on expertise suggests that a superficial coverage of many topics in the domain may be a poor way to help students develop the competencies that will prepare them for future learning and work. Curricula that emphasize breadth of knowledge may prevent effective organization of knowledge because there is not enough time to learn anything in depth. Curricula that are a "mile wide and an inch deep" run the risk of developing disconnected rather than connected knowledge.

5.3

Understanding by Design Template

Stage 1—Identify Desired Results

Established Goal(s)
• What relevant goals (e.g., content standards, course or program objectives, learning outcomes) will this design address?

Understanding(s)	**Essential Question(s)**
• What are the "big ideas"?	• What provocative questions will foster
• What specific understandings about them are	inquiry, understanding, and transfer of
desired?	learning?
• What misunderstandings are predictable?	

Students will know . . . . Students will be able to . . . .
• What key knowledge and skills will students acquire as a result of this unit?
• What should they eventually be able to do as a result of such knowledge and skill?

Stage 2—Determine Acceptable Evidence

Performance Task(s)	**Other Evidence**
• Through what authentic performance task(s)	• Through what other evidence (e.g., quizzes,
will students demonstrate the desired	tests, academic prompts, observations, home-
understandings?	work, journals) will students demonstrate
• By what criteria will performances of under-	achievement of the desired results?
standing be judged?	• How will students reflect upon and
	self-assess their own learning?

Stage 3—Plan Learning Experiences and Instruction

Learning Activities
What learning experiences and instruction will enable students to achieve the desired results? How will the design—

    W = help the students know **where** the unit is going and **what** is expected? Help the teacher know **where** the students are coming from (prior knowledge, interests)?
    H = **hook** all students and **hold** their interest?
    E = **equip** students, help them **experience** the key ideas and **explore** the issues?
    R = provide opportunities to **rethink** and **revise** their understandings and work?
    E = allow students to **evaluate** their work and its implications?
    T = be **tailored** (personalized) to the different needs, interests, and abilities of learners?
    O = be **organized** to maximize initial and sustained engagement as well as effective learning?

Source: Adapted with permission from *Understanding by Design* by Grant Wiggins and Jay McTighe, 1998, Alexandria, VA: Association for Supervision and Curriculum Development.

Wiggins and McTighe (1998) also advocate "critical review" of curriculum through both the peer review process and feedback from students. Peer review (against established design standards) not only helps teachers to refine their understanding of the model but also facilitates important conversations around key questions at "the heart of teaching and learning":

> ➤ What is worthy of understanding in this unit?
> ➤ What counts as evidence that students really understand and can use what we're teaching?
> ➤ What knowledge and skills must we teach to enable them to apply their knowledge in meaningful ways? (p. 179)

Curriculum mapping provides members of the school community with two different "lenses" for looking at curriculum: "a zoom lens into this year's curriculum for a particular grade and a wide-angle lens to see the K–12 perspective" (Jacobs, 1997, p. 3). The value of these dual lenses is that they provide a means to gather data for what is taught, when it is taught, and how it is assessed. This picture of both the classroom level and the school/district level provides key insights in several important areas:

> ➤ Gaps and repetitions in content among teachers on the same grade level and across grade levels
> ➤ Areas of emphasis and gaps between the local curriculum and the state standards
> ➤ Big ideas/concepts that are transferable over time (across grades, across subjects, in the "real world")
> ➤ Range of assessment vehicles used to evaluate student work

After the curriculum maps are drafted, they also provide powerful opportunities to (1) refine (and sometimes redefine) what students are expected to know and be able to do and (2) consider how those expectations serve as a bridge to both where the students have just been (last year) and where they are headed (next year). Jacobs (1997) affirms this point:

Curriculum mapping offers the opportunity to scrutinize our current practice with an eye to the spiraling nature of the learner's experience over time. In fact, the greatest value of mapping comes when teams of teachers review maps to determine the appropriate match between the level of student learning and the type of work expected. (p. 36)

These conversations result in not only greater teacher clarity about the purposefulness of the work but also a more complex, richer conception of collective curriculum. When school staff have a more informed conception of curriculum, a teacher's daily decisions about how to deliver instruction not only affects student achievement in that classroom but also future student achievement, for it is assumed that students will be entering the next classroom prepared to handle a more sophisticated or more expansive level of work.

It is important to emphasize once again that the content of the staff development program is less relevant to this book than the process used for determining the content and design. *Understanding by Design* and curriculum mapping are popular and powerful innovations, but they represent only one way to close the gap. The staff also could have focused on any number of innovations, including:

➤ The design and implementation of a literacy program to ensure that students received targeted instruction in reading and writing in every classroom
➤ The design and implementation of a series of performance tasks and common rubrics that are in alignment with the state assessment
➤ The design and implementation of technology training to ensure that students had the opportunity, ability, and access to use technology to advance their work

Regardless of what innovations are selected, the innovations are in service to the system, not the other way around. That is why the discussion in earlier chapters about establishing a shared vision, articulating what the shared vision looks like when it is put into practice, using data to identify current performance levels, and identifying the gaps between current performance and ideal performance are crucial to the ultimate success of a continuous improvement effort.

Staff Conversation #9

At the next faculty meeting, Joan gives the staff a quick refresher on the agreed-upon plan of action and identifies the volunteers who established the links between *Understanding by Design*, curriculum mapping, and the school vision statement. She then turns the floor over to Ann, who is emerging as a key leader in this innovation.

Ann: What we did first was to brainstorm the key concerns with the original curriculum map template from several years ago. This discussion was grounded in the feedback you gave us at the last faculty meeting (Figure 5.2, p. 113).

Ann displays a large chart that shows components of the original curriculum map, the related concerns expressed by staff, and components of the revised curriculum map that would address those concerns (Figure 5.4, p. 124). She continues her presentation.

Ann: As you can see from the revised map that we are proposing, it is in strong alignment with *Understanding by Design*. In fact, the proposed format includes all fields in Stages 1 and 2 of the UBD template. After we thought through the relationship between the two innovations, we then compared the proposed format to our vision statements developed last spring.

Ann displays a second chart that shows the linkage between the vision statements and the proposed innovations (Figure 5.5, p. 126).

Ann: Based on this analysis, we're convinced that moving forward with curriculum mapping and *Understanding by Design* will be enormously effective in closing gaps between the vision and where we are now. There are, however, two gaps that we'll need to address in the mid to long term, but we

5.4

Moving from Original to Suggested Curriculum Map Template

Original Curriculum Map	Key Concerns	Revised Curriculum Map
Time of year	• Calendar is a good-faith effort to keep parents up-to-date but can quickly become obsolete because of student needs, pacing issues, and other issues. Result may create more confusion than guidance for parents.	**Time frame (# of weeks)** Provides more flexibility so that the time line serves as a guideline for parents, not a calendar.
Topics/content	• No framework is provided to suggest why topics are covered or how they fit into a larger vision of what students are expected to know and be able to do.	**State content standards** Illustrates alignment between curriculum and state expectations about what students are expected to know and be able to do.
Concepts	• There's a lack of clarity about whether this should list all concepts or key ones. • Based on how the box is being completed, there's a lack of clarity about what constitutes a concept.	**Big ideas** These are the core concepts, principles, theories, and processes at the heart of the subject area/grade level curricula.
		Essential questions These provide the lens through which students explore the big ideas, knowledge, and skills in the unit. The questions are open-ended and require reasoning and justification (rather than a "right" answer). They also naturally recur across grades (and can recur across subject areas).

5.4 *(continued)*
Moving from Original to Suggested Curriculum Map Template

Original Curriculum Map	Key Concerns	Revised Curriculum Map
Skills	• There's a lack of clarity about whether this should list all skills or key ones. • Also need to make sure that this supports the content standards but doesn't simply copy sections from them.	**What students should know** This outlines key knowledge that students will be expected to demonstrate on assessments. **What students should be able to do** This outlines key skills that students will be expected to be able to use on assessments.
Major assessments	• Many maps repeat general titles such as "Chapter test and quiz," which offer little insight as to what the assessment will measure and what those measurement tools will look like. • Changes in calendar may create confusion about due dates.	**Performance task(s)** These assessments require students to apply their knowledge and skills in a new (and authentic) situation. **Other evidence** These assessments directly measure whether students can demonstrate key knowledge and skills.
(None)	• Need to identify sources for data collection that can be used to evaluate student achievement across classrooms.	**Core assessments** These assessments are outside of the unit format to indicate culminating tools to evaluate learning across multiple units. They can be either locally designed by our staff or externally designed (e.g., state or national assessments).

Source: Adapted from work completed in Nanuet Public Schools, Nanuet, NY.

5.5

How Our Vision and Proposed Innovations Are Linked

Shared Vision	Curriculum Mapping and Understanding by Design
• I will see classroom instruction dominated by questions and explorations, not lecture.	• Essential questions are identified on curriculum map. • Asking questions and articulating answers dominate classroom conversation.
• I will see instruction that focuses on discovering the concepts that lie at the heart of each discipline and how the concept is an inference about the relationship among items of knowledge in the discipline.	• Big ideas are identified on curriculum map.
• I will hear students, in class discussion and performance, making connections among discrete pieces of knowledge and/or skill and then regularly revisiting these inferences to check for their continued adequacy. When an inference is found to be inadequate, I will hear students reflect and revise to accommodate new data arising from new learning.	• Use of big ideas and essential questions over time (both vertically and horizontally) ensures connections and inferences. • Curriculum map prioritizes what is most important for students to know and be able to do. • Student understandings are established and refined by design: unit and lesson plans are designed to make this happen.
• I will see evidence that students do well at tests of knowledge, measures of performance on open-ended prompts, and challenges requiring the use of knowledge and skill in new, important, and authentic ways.	• Performance tasks and other evidence appear on curriculum map.
• I will see a consistently high level of student achievement across this variety of assessment instruments.	• Locally designed core assessments as well as externally designed state and national assessments are listed on curriculum map.
• I will see curricula and classrooms that are organized around problems. The content of the course becomes the means for solving the problem.	• Performance-based assessments are included on curriculum map.

5.5 *(continued)*

How Our Vision and Proposed Innovations Are Linked

Shared Vision	Curriculum Mapping and Understanding by Design
• I will see classrooms where students consistently raise the established essential questions that are designed to be the guide for learning.	• Essential questions are included on curriculum map.
• I will hear students who can explain the importance of the learning they are engaged in and how it will be of future value to them. This explanation is not in platitudes but instead reflects a clear grasp of the transfer value of the learning.	• Because of increased teacher clarity on curriculum and instruction through the completion of curriculum maps, the students will be clearer as well.
• I will see a classroom that emphasizes the development and evaluation of multiple problem-solving strategies, identifying the most promising and being adaptable as the strategies are tested.	• Strategies can be built into both performance assessments and other evidence fields on template.
• I will see students competently use knowledge and skill in new, important ways to solve realistic problems.	• Opportunities for self-assessment are built into the lesson plans. • Performance assessment is included on curriculum map.
• I will see a clear rubric for scoring excellence for every product or performance students are asked to generate. • I will see a common set of school rubrics for the same traits in performance used consistently across teachers and subjects. In cases in which rubrics must be discipline specific, the faculty will agree to this modification, and the students will understand the reason for the required modification.	• Will need to do rubric development after curriculum-mapping initiative is underway. Will bundle starting next year or year after. This will require outside help and significant allocation of resources. (same as above)

5.5 *(continued)*

How Our Vision and Proposed Innovations Are Linked

Shared Vision	Curriculum Mapping and Understanding by Design
• I will see students who can apply the school's rubrics to their own work and to the work of peers and assess at a high level of reliability with the score assigned by the teacher.	(same as above)
• I will see curriculum that sets high standards for all students, instruction and teacher communication that foster the meeting of these standards, and a rich variety of assessments that provides students the opportunity to demonstrate mastery. • I will see a common set of school rubrics for the same traits in performance used consistently across teachers and subjects. • I will see students internalizing high standards and revising their work to come closer to meeting such standards.	• All curriculum maps will be in strong alignment with state standards and will target key knowledge and skill areas. • Time frame on curriculum map increases consistency in curriculum across classrooms. • Rubrics will be bundled into staff development beginning next year or year after. (same as above)
• I will see curriculum that articulates key concepts, content, and skills that are necessary for all students to learn and instruction targeted to ensure all students learn these essentials. • I will see school programs being implemented that prepare all students for learning and success. • I will see all students having equitable access to all educational programs.	• Curriculum map will be done for all grade levels and all subjects. • All curriculum maps will be in strong alignment with state standards and will target key knowledge and skill areas. (same as above) • We hold all students to the same standards; we differentiate how we assess and design learning experiences.

recommend they not be addressed this year: rubric development and development of our own mandated core assessments. Although these are an integral part of the work we need to do, we think that it may be too difficult to try to do this while we're beginning our work on *Understanding by Design* and curriculum mapping. Two additional areas for further examination and staff development are (1) more effectively communicating to students the purposefulness of the work, and (2) developing multiple problem-solving strategies to make students more independent and flexible thinkers. We have no recommendation as to whether these two additional points can be handled in the short term or if we should postpone emphasis on them until the refinement stage of our work. When it happens isn't as important as that it happens.

The staff meeting is opened up so participants can provide feedback and ask questions. The questions reflect a variety of concerns:

➤ *When are we going to learn all of this stuff? I can't do this during the school year and give the time I need to my students!*

➤ *How is this map going to "match" our resources? Do current resources drive the map or will the map drive what resources we use? Does this mean that textbook adoption will be driven by the map? Will it slow down that process?*

➤ *Whom are the maps for? And how does the audience for the maps influence what (and how much) we write?*

➤ *Are we responsible for creating and using the same map as other teachers who have the same subject area and grade level of students? How do we come to consensus on what should be in the maps? When will we have time to debrief with each other the problems or issues that come up during implementation?*

➤ *How will we measure whether the maps affect student achievement? What should we be able to see? How do we know what we can attribute to the innovation? It seems difficult to isolate this as the variable that makes a difference.*

➤ *How often do we need to reopen the map? It isn't so bad if we have to go through this process only once, but I don't think I have the time, energy, or interest to do it every year.*

➤ *Will there be a point at which we can revisit what the template has on it?*
What if we find that certain boxes aren't working? Or that we're missing
information? Can one teacher or a group of teachers add more information
on their maps without affecting all of the teachers in the building?

Joan validates the importance of the questions but also provides little in the
way of answers. She promises that these issues will be addressed, both individually and collectively, but that now is not the time. The meeting adjourns,
and staff members file out of the room, somewhat confused about whether
their concerns have been dismissed because of their complexity or because it
wasn't the right time to go into that much detail. Right after the faculty meeting, Joan asks Ann to stay for a couple of minutes to debrief.

Ann: How do you think it went? I thought the staff asked some really
tough questions.

Joan: Your job was to show the faculty how curriculum mapping, *Understanding by Design*, and our shared vision are all interrelated. Although their
questions were good, notice that all accepted the linkage as evident, and they
were asking questions about how to "do it."

Ann: I think the staff left with a clear picture of where we are headed but
have some serious reservations about whether this time it will be different—
meaning that this time all participants will get the training, support, and time
they need to do this work well. It would be deadly to have created such a
well-grounded, well-intentioned vision and then return to "old habits" for
how we implement change in the building.

Joan: That raises an important question that I've had. Why didn't you
come to me three years ago when we did curriculum mapping the first time? I
know that I wasn't as aware of systems thinking as I am now, but I still believe
that I was approachable and accessible. If you needed more time or more clarity about the form and function of the original curriculum maps, why didn't
you ask for it?

Ann: *[Smiling]* The reason I didn't say something back then was that I
believed that staff development was an imposition or an obligation, not an
opportunity to grow. It was something that I "did" because I was told to do it;
your agenda, not mine. I too have now become more of a systems thinker, and

that has changed what I see as the parameters of my job and my responsibility to you and the rest of the staff.

Joan: And now?

Ann: The biggest change for me over the past six months is that I now trust that the interesting conversations about what "ought to be" have become our collective agenda. This makes change feel a lot slower and more belabored (like some of the work we did last year), but, looking back on it now, I'm amazed not only by the clarity we've achieved but also that we've gotten to this point together. Let me assure you that I won't hesitate to talk to you in the future about concerns, both mine and others', to make sure we continue to build upon where we are; and that these conversations will be in the development phase as opposed to waiting for a public forum.

Joan: I really value both your willingness to speak frankly with me about the effectiveness of current teaching and learning practices and our efforts to improve them. You also have a way of articulating your position so that your colleagues can understand what it looks like—or doesn't look like—in practice and can imagine its potential value.

Ann: Thanks, Joan. I really have enjoyed working as a partner with you in this.

Joan: Would you be interested in formalizing this partnership?

Joan and Ann begin to discuss the details of forming a "change facilitator team." They agree to meet later in the week to talk in more depth and to begin planning strategically to implement this innovation. They also identify Susan as someone who would bring an important perspective to the conversation because of her insistence on evidence that this innovation is the "right fit" for the school's vision.

Analysis of Staff Conversation #9

Joan has been very clear for some time now that she can't "go it alone" when it comes to implementing change. She has created various staff teams or committees over the past two years, but for the first time she is specifically designating staff members and formalizing those relationships in something referred to as a "change facilitator team." This concept was coined by Hall and Hord (2001) to describe the team who leads the implementation effort. Each member of the team understands that there is a "hierarchical relationship [among] them in a supervisory sense, [but] they approach the change facilitation job as a partnership" (p. 151). This partnership stems from sharing "information about what teachers are doing and [jointly analyzing] their successes, concerns, and needs" (p. 151). The change facilitator team consists of three roles: first change facilitator (Joan), second change facilitator (Ann), and third change facilitator (Susan).

The first change facilitator is the official leader of the change effort: the principal in the case of a building-based change innovation, the superintendent or assistant superintendent in the case of a district-based innovation. In this instance, the formal leader of the effort is Joan.

The second change facilitator is typically either an assistant principal or a teacher leader. The second change facilitator must be both a trusted confidant of the first change facilitator and be viewed as accessible and important in the eyes of the staff. This is what Rogers (1995) labels "*an opinion leader,* an individual whom [other teachers] trust and turn to for advice and information about the innovation" (as cited in Hall & Hord, 2001, p. 150). This person's role is to assist in both the planning and the implementation of the change. Joan has selected Ann to function in this capacity.

The third change facilitator plays a less formal role in the planning and implementation of the change. This person is trusted to bring expertise as well as a different and valued perspective that adds needed complexity and depth to both the planning and implementation steps (Hall & Hord, 2001). Susan has been identified for this role because of her steadfast and valuable position on the importance of closing the gaps that have been identified and the emerging respect she has earned from her colleagues for staying committed to what they all value.

This change facilitator team will become an integral part of the implementation, monitoring, and adjusting of the staff development program so that the change is both powerful and pervasive. By broadening the circle of responsibility for the change effort, Joan will more likely be able to provide the support her staff needs during the change process.

It is clear that Joan and her staff have achieved consensus around the direction of a substantial staff development undertaking. However, they have largely done this in isolation from the rest of the district. In her excitement about the transformation of her school and the fast pace of the past few weeks, Joan has lost sight of the link between the school and the district. The assumption that staff development can be self-generated not only is misleading to staff but untenable to district personnel who think systemically. Joan will be reminded of this point once again at the principals' meeting the next afternoon.

Administrator Conversation #4

The October principals' meeting has just one item on the agenda: implementation of a new K–12 math framework. The principals are not surprised that the framework has been developed, but they are taken aback by the mandate that this be implemented immediately. Many of the principals are in the same boat as Joan; they have established a school-based agenda that will require most of the available time for staff development work.

After the meeting, Joan decides to ask Ed to make an exception for her school. When she walks down the hallway to Ed's office, she overhears one of her colleagues lobbying Ed for the same thing.

Dave: Come on, Ed. Our school is already overburdened without throwing this on top of the pile. How can you expect us to implement this framework on top of the emphasis on conflict resolution? I can't very well pull the math teachers out from that conversation, especially after some of the serious problems we had last year. If you don't let us finish that first, we'll wind up doing neither innovation well.

Ed: I hear your point, but there's nothing I can do. First, this is important work that has been a long time coming and that shouldn't have come to you as a surprise today. Second, this is a mandate from the superintendent and the board. You and your math teachers will be working with this framework and with the support of this office so that implementation will be successful.

➤

Dave leaves, clearly upset. Joan's intention to ask for a delay is no longer an option. However, she knows that she has to deal with this issue now. If she doesn't inform her staff quickly, they will hear about the mandate from their colleagues in other buildings, and that would undermine the collegiality she has been working so hard to develop among her staff.

Ed: *[Muttering to himself]* Damn. Some principals are just blockers.

Joan: *[Knocking lightly on the open door to Ed's office]* Can we talk for a minute?

Ed: Look, Joan, don't start in on me, too. I know your staff is busy setting their own agenda; but remember, Henry warned you that your school is part of this district and has to meet district priorities, not just your parochial vision. If this is about an extension, you're wasting your time.

Joan: I know that we need to do this. We're part of the system, and we have a responsibility to make the math framework functional this year. But I need you to help me find a way to bundle this district innovation with the complex school-based changes we're already committed to implementing this year. Ann is serving as a partner in the change process in the building. Would you come by and meet with both of us to address this issue?

Ed: *[Sounding skeptical]* As long as you're serious about working on both agendas. I just don't want to have the debate again over whose agenda is more important.

Joan briefs Ann the next day about the math framework. Three days later, Ed, Joan, and Ann meet after school to discuss how to bundle the innovations without jeopardizing either agenda. Once they sit down with both the math framework and the curriculum map template in front of them, it becomes apparent that the math framework already contains key information for several of the boxes on the curriculum map. What also becomes clear, however, is that the math teachers in Joan's building will need to receive training and support on the origin of the math framework; the process used by the K–12 math framework to identify concepts, knowledge, and skills; and specific instructions so that the curriculum maps that are produced mirror (and potentially supplement) the findings of that committee.

Ed: I really see how what you're working on here is going to serve the interest of the district as a whole, even if it wasn't designed that way. I want to acknowledge this by saying that the district will support your building innovations conceptually and financially.

Joan: You always do, Ed.

Ed: But the support doesn't come without a price. I expect you to report back to me regularly. You know what you're undertaking is certainly worthwhile but definitely not easy.

Ann: That's why we're so glad this is a district- and school-supported effort. We're going to need the resources to be able to bring people to the building to provide the training that teachers need in order to do these maps right. They can't just fill in the boxes without really understanding what the concepts mean and how they function in curriculum.

Ed: Like I said, I'm willing to underwrite this, but this is only part of what I was trying to say. The other part is not financial but rather involves careful planning so that you can help teachers where they need it, when they need it. It's not a resource allocation issue alone.

Ann: What do you mean?

Ed: You can anticipate what the responses of your teachers are going to be to this innovation and then plan for them.

Ann: I still don't understand what you mean. I think the teachers are really behind the work we're trying to accomplish.

Ed: Don't confuse support for the idea with ease of implementation. Almost 20 years ago, a group of researchers articulated a framework for thinking about predictable stages of concern teachers experience in the change process. Hall and Hord called it the Concerns-Based Adoption Model, or CBAM. It's one of these things that has been around for a while but has not lost its power or its relevance. I particularly recommend that you and Joan talk through these stages so that you can tailor staff development and target resources based on where people are.

Joan: I remember looking at the CBAM stuff years ago when I was getting my administrator certification, but I haven't thought about it in a long time. We could really use your help on this one, Ed—nothing better than an expert right here at home.

➤

Ann: And if the stages are as predictable as you say they are, there really is a value to having you become part of the change facilitator team.

Because of the district commitment to the innovation, Joan can set up a contract with Tom, an *Understanding by Design* consultant, to work with her staff on a long-term basis. This is crucial to the change process because it allows Joan to build a long-term relationship with one consultant and gives him the opportunity to get to know her staff and her school, thereby tailoring his work more closely to the school culture. His expertise and the envisioned relationship make him an "external change facilitator."

Ed also becomes an external change facilitator because of his expertise in implementing change. Not only does he bring a K–12 perspective to the table, but he also will make sure that the change process is in alignment with district accountability to the state. His background in CBAM will help the internal change facilitators as they work to manage a host of concerns inherent in the change process.

Analysis of Administrator Conversation #4

The relationship between the school and the district has been touched upon throughout the book, but for the first time in the evolution of the change process, it poses a significant obstacle to the continuous improvement effort. In districts across the country, it is likely that central office mandates are expected to function in concert with school-based change efforts regardless of how much the two connect. When administrators disagree about what is worth spending time on, the reform effort is likely to be as fleeting as the enforcement pressures (Darling-Hammond, 1997). However, "top-down" mandates can provide the leverage that leaders need to institute change. Central office is more than a clearinghouse for mandates.

> Although mandates are continually criticized as being ineffective because of their top-down orientation, they can work quite well. With a mandate the priority is clear, and there is an expectation that the innovation will be implemented. The mandating process falls down, however, when the only time the change process is supported is at the initial announcement of the mandate. When a mandate is

accompanied by continuing communication, ongoing training, on-site coaching, and time for implementation, it can operate quite well. As with most change strategies, the mandate has gotten a bad name not because the strategy itself is flawed but because it is not supported with the other interventions that are necessary. (Hall & Hord, 2001, p. 14)

Based on the number of innovations that have entered and exited Joan's school prior to this latest effort and the negative attitude of the staff on staff development days, it is reasonable to infer that the needed interventions were not made. It also is evident, based on how the math framework has been introduced to the principals, that central office administrators have identified the desired result (that these frameworks be integrated into every building's math program) but offer no support on how to achieve such integration. The same dilemmas raised in earlier chapters about individual autonomy apply here among the various buildings in the district. It is likely that the schools within this district will each do "something" with the math frameworks but with little knowledge or accountability as to what that work looks like in other buildings and with little clarity on whether their work has produced the desired results. Ed begins to realize that he needs Joan and her staff to serve as a model of what successful implementation of this mandate could look like. On a more profound level, Ed begins to recognize that he, too, will need to go through a similar envisioning process from the vantage point of the district as a system. Although that journey is not the focus of this book, it is clear that the same operating principles apply.

When building-based administrators enlist the leadership and support of district-based administrators, central office becomes an integral part of the change process. Hall and Hord (2001) advocate that schools need this outside support from the district.

The school can and must do a lot by itself, but it also needs to move in concert with and be supported by the other components of the system. . . . Change is a complex, dynamic, and resource-consuming endeavor. No single organization, be it a school or national corporation, is likely to have all the expertise and resources needed to succeed in change. (p. 14)

The partnership between the school and the central office makes it possible for Joan to add two final people to the change facilitator team, both of whom will serve as external change facilitators. External change facilitators can provide "expert knowledge about the innovation," function as key "liaisons" between the school and external organizations, update the internal facilitation team on how staff are functioning and what they need (both individually and collectively), and serve as a "sounding board" for ideas and problem solving (Hall & Hord, 2001, pp. 153–154).

Summing Up and Looking Ahead

The status quo of isolation that has characterized the job descriptions of so many educators in this system has begun to be eradicated from the culture. As a result of their collective work in the opening days of school, teachers see that they are trusted to make decisions about the direction and scope of the change effort. The creation of a change facilitator team brings teachers and administrators together to develop a plan that will institute the innovation in a way that differentiates resources and entry points for individuals and still holds all staff accountable for growing over time. The range of roles on the change facilitator team helps teachers to get feedback and guidance and helps administrators feel more connected to the work of the staff. This enables them to function more as instructional leaders instead of just building managers. Another important development is the more direct partnership between district-level and building-based administrators. The district-level administrators rely on the school staff to implement K–12 innovations, but they also are learning the value of grassroots development of change. Joan and her staff appreciate that they need district resources to support their ambitious plans.

The change facilitator team's next step: The members of the team must meet to develop a long-term action plan that outlines the key steps of implementation. They must then present this plan to all members of the school community to give them clarity on the big picture.

The reader's next step: With your school and your district in mind, consider the following questions:

➤ How do we design and implement a staff development program that will help to close the gaps between our vision and reality?

➤ Do we have too many changes going on at one time? Too few? How do we know? Who "owns" them?

➤ Who is leading? Is the leadership structure effective? Why? Why not? What's the evidence?

➤ Are leadership and facilitation synonymous? Should they be? Why?

➤ What are the concerns of staff? What new ones can be anticipated? Can any of them be avoided? Minimized? How? By whom?

➤ What role do directives from the state, the board of education, or the central office play in our change efforts? Why? Should there be a larger role? A smaller role? Is the answer the same for all change efforts? Why?

6

Developing an Action Plan

Essential Question

How do we make it happen?

Operating Principles

—Staff development must promote collective autonomy by embracing teaching as a distributed quality of the school.

— Planning must provide the clear, concrete direction necessary for systemic change while remaining flexible enough to accommodate the "nonrational" life in schools.

—Staff development must reflect the predictable stages of teacher concern about the complexities of moving from new learning to systemic consequences.

Chapter Overview

This chapter focuses on step five of continuous improvement: the development and implementation of an action plan that addresses teacher concerns and results in integration of the innovations throughout the school and within each classroom. The basis of this chapter, however, goes far beyond practical guidelines for action planning; the conversation and analysis are grounded in how to organize staff development in a way that enables a culture of collective autonomy. Staff who think about students through the dual lens of "my" students in "my" class (this year) and "our" students in "our" program (for the amount of time the students are a part of the system) make it possible for the system to perform better as a result of the collective endeavors. At this phase of development of a competent system, teaching must become a "distributive quality" (McDonald, 1996), whereby success is measured not by the efforts of individual teachers but by the performance of the school as a whole.

Therefore, the change facilitator team must develop an action plan that includes the following three characteristics:

➤ Addresses practical questions such as time lines, resources needed to support staff, organizational changes to facilitate the process, budgetary constraints, and communication with key stakeholders.

➤ Establishes observable indicators to measure what it will look like when the innovations are being successfully implemented as well as key points of growth along the way.

➤ Plans for predictable concerns (and be open to unpredictable ones) that will arise during the change process.

The focus of action planning is always on moving the innovation to a higher, more refined level (Hall & Hord, 2001; Glickman, 1993). Because of this and the resulting systemic consequences, a key factor in its success is the effectiveness of the planning and facilitation process: poor planning and facilitation can seriously damage the school as a system, entrenching its incompetence; on the other hand, thoughtful planning can bring to fruition the characteristics of a competent system already discussed (see Figure 2.2 in Chapter 2).

Staff reflection #1

It's Friday night and Ann sets the alarm clock for 5:30 a.m. Although she isn't thrilled that she is going to be getting up so early on a Saturday morning, this is the only time the change facilitator team is able to meet before Thanksgiving. She is looking forward to the opportunity to spend two uninterrupted days ironing out the details of an action plan for the staff development work. As she gets ready, she thinks about the work ahead:

I've never been on the development end of an action plan before. Prior to this year I only saw the action plan in its finalized form where what I was expected to do was clearly defined. It's more familiar to be a recipient, even if the plan seemed to me to be superficial or flawed or not worthy of the effort. Now that I have the opportunity to make sure that the plan is connected to the "real work" of teachers, I am not sure if I know how to make this happen.

Ann begins to think about the purpose of their action plan—an increase in student achievement:

But if there is going to be higher achievement, there needs to be higher quality teaching. Is it my job tomorrow to define how all of my colleagues are going to be changed? This idea of having responsibility for "fixing" my colleagues makes me very uncomfortable—like I know what is better for them than they do. Haven't our conversations always been about how do we fix the school as a system? Maybe I need to think of teaching not in terms of any one individual, but instead what is expected from us as a group.

Analysis of staff reflection #1

Ann's reflection illustrates an emerging realization that teaching is a "distributed quality," quantifiably based on the achievement of all students rather than the achievement of "my" students. Although this appears new to Ann, two well-known researchers have challenged the conventional notion that teaching is a "highly individualized practice." McDonald (1996) reports:

> Our study convinced us that good schools depend on good teaching but that good teaching is best thought of as a distributed property—a quality of schools rather than teachers. Our evidence is that good teaching is more stable, reliable, and pervasive when groups of people rather than individuals are expected to supply it (p. 106).

Marzano (2003) reached a similar conclusion in his synthesis of research on the effects on student achievement of school and teacher effectiveness. This meta-analysis shows that when teaching is effective and the school is effective, students entering at the 50th percentile achieve at the 96th percentile after two years (p. 75). To build a competent system, it is useful to think of good teaching as a property of both teachers and schools.

As the change facilitator team begins to hammer out the details for implementing the bundled innovations, they must also be mindful of how to cultivate a culture of collective autonomy. Staff must have clarity on why the staff development plan is a viable means to close the gap between the shared vision and reality; they must be clear on what successful implementation looks like; they must be empowered to share their concerns and measure their own growth over time; and they must be accountable to the principal and one another for implementing the change.

Change Facilitator Team Conversation #1

It is seven o'clock on that Saturday morning as Joan pulls into the parking lot, anxious and excited about the next two days' work. Armed with flip charts, markers, a computer, apples, and a bag of chocolates, Joan heads inside for what is sure to be a powerful, productive, and exhausting day.

Joan, Ann, and Susan begin the work of the day by asking: what do we expect staff to know, be able to do, and understand in two years? They quickly agree that the top priority is to complete the curriculum maps so that there will be a clear picture of the scope and sequence for each subject area.

The conversation is an intense brainstorming session where deliberation about one idea triggers deliberation about another idea, proving the complex interaction of elements within a system. They begin with the idea that:

> Staff must receive rigorous training by subject area. That will make the training concrete enough in theory and give teachers access to the richness of collective thinking as they work to achieve consensus on what students must learn—knowledge, skills, and understanding. But, based on the size of the staff and available resources, it will likely take two years just to get all of the teachers through this kind of training experience. The time line should be expanded to three to five years. Although this targeted training will provide guidance specific to the subject area, it will take more than that for staff to visualize how the

curriculum map will affect daily instruction. How does this find its way into instructional practice?

➤ If staff members are going to see the connection between the units on the subject-area maps and the day-to-day learning experiences they design for students, they must have the opportunity to develop lessons. They will then need to talk in subject-area teams to determine the alignment between the daily work and the overall vision of the map. But two other key alignment issues must be discussed: alignment among subject areas on the same grade level and alignment in the same subject area across grade levels. To effectively spiral the curriculum, teachers must have easy access to each other's curriculum maps. But how is this access to be provided?

➤ To give teachers access to each other's maps, the school must set up a database to house the curriculum maps and the units of instruction. This will make it easier for staff to see curriculum systemically, which in turn should lead to refinements in the maps and in instruction. But how will we know, even if aligned, that the maps are working?

➤ It is clear that student assessment data will be the primary way to evaluate the maps.

Having worked into the afternoon, the team decides to call it a day and individually reflect on the work before they begin anew. On the following day, the team picks up the conversation, this time with Ed, who only was able to join them on the second day. They begin by reviewing for Ed the key points raised the previous day.

➤ Ed adds a suggestion that the effectiveness of the maps must also be judged on whether they are in alignment with the state standards and the new district math framework. Ed suggests that, because this analysis will be such an important evaluation of the work of the school, it should be shared with members of the school community.

➤ The school will need to report student achievement annually to staff, parents, board members, and community members. This report will not only include external testing data mandated by the state but also will need to go well beyond that to include (1) the results of locally designed assessments that measure the sophistication of student knowledge, skills, and understanding; (2) an analysis of programmatic reasons for any weaknesses in achievement; and (3) plans to revise program to remedy current weaknesses and to avoid them in the future. Will Joan have the time necessary to oversee such an ambitious and complex change process, given all of her other day-to-day responsibilities?

➤ Ed suggests that if Ann could teach part-time each day or be released from her class one day a week, she could use the time to help facilitate the change process. This would make the leadership task much more doable. What other school policies, procedures, and regulations will we need to reconsider in light of this change process?

➤ The bundled innovations are going to have a ripple effect. It may change teacher schedules so that they have common planning time. It may require a more detailed report card system so that it is clear what the grades on student report cards really indicate. But who is the audience for the report cards?

➤ If we are going to make changes on this large a scale, we have to involve parents and other members of the school community in these conversations. This is more than a public relations campaign to get them to support the kinds of reforms we are trying to undertake. How are we going to fund this work over the next three to five years?

➤ Although it is relatively easy to set aside money for now, it is likely that next year or the year after, staff or other administrators will be intrigued by a new innovation, and the tendency may be to pull back the support of this one to accommodate the next one. Ed raises another point.

➤ We need a concrete tool to measure collective growth in curriculum and instructional practices. Ed suggests that, if the team members can develop such a measurement tool, they would be able to collect data on where staff are in the implementation of the staff development and to target human and financial resources to ensure future growth. Such a continuum will need to be clear in defining predictable stages of implementation for the innovation—answering the questions "What does a novice look like?" "What does the more skilled practitioner look like?" and so on. Ed suggests that Tom (their *Understanding by Design* consultant) help with the development of this tool because of his extensive expertise with implementing the innovation in a number of schools. How can an action plan ever capture this degree of complexity?

➤ The action plan we need to develop will be our best answer today but may not be the best answer tomorrow. The plan will need to be evolutionary and flexible based on new issues, new ideas, new needs, or new data that emerge as the change is being implemented. We will need to have this kind of retreat twice a year to revisit the plan and to make necessary revisions and adjustments.

With only three hours remaining in the marathon planning session, the change facilitator team begins to translate the brainstorming session into a concrete action plan. The first phase of the plan (See Figure 6.1, p. 148) concerns the completion of the curriculum maps.

➤ Susan agrees to enlist the school's technology department to help her customize a software program that will allow teachers to input their curriculum maps into an established format and give staff members access to the maps on line. She commits to having this done by March 1st.

➤ Ed and Joan agree to tackle the job of developing action plans for addressing school policies and procedures. They will share these plans in two weeks time and meet to finalize them within two more weeks.

➤ Ed agrees to take to the superintendent the proposal for a change in Ann's teaching duties. He will do this next week.

➤ The full team will meet in April to revisit ideas raised in the brainstorming session that are not part of the first phase of the action plan.

Analysis of Change Facilitator Team Conversation #1

The members of the change facilitator team have individually expressed their determination and dedication to this continuous improvement effort, but the preceding conversation was the first time they collectively established a practical, functional, and feasible approach to make that happen. Although the part of the action plan drafted at the end of the weekend session is refreshingly concrete, the brainstorming conversations that led to the action plan may have appeared somewhat baffling both in their relationships and in their scope. These excerpts, which are only some of the many ideas that likely arose during the hours of conversation, validate the operating principle from Chapter 2: *Each school is a complex, living system with purpose.* As Sarason (1990) explains: "What you seek to change is so embedded in a system of interacting parts that if it is changed, then changes elsewhere are likely to occur" (p. 16). Staff development does produce a change to existing teaching and learning practices, which, in turn, will impact the entire system in predictable and unpredictable ways.

At this juncture, the change facilitator team has planned for the ripple effect that this one change will have on other interrelated parts of the system in a way that is both politically and economically feasible. The format of the action plan excerpt presented in Figure 6.1 is a typical organizational template used to outline actions, responsibilities, time lines, and evidence that the action is completed. While a plan, such as this one, must be comprehensive, it also must be revisited over time to ensure that it can accommodate the "nonrational" life of a system. Pascale et al. explain "living systems cannot be directed along a linear path. Unforseen consequences are inevitable"(as cited in Fullan 2001, p. 45). Therefore, leaders must be careful not to make enforcement of the original plan an end unto itself; "The goal of strategic planning is to produce a stream of wise decisions . . . it also accepts the possibility that the final product may not resemble what was initially intended" (Patterson, Purkey, & Parker, as cited in Fullan & Stiegelbauer, 1991, p. 108).

Moving Toward Successful Implementation

To ensure "wise decisions," two key concepts inform both the initial development of the plan and its modification: the innovation configuration map and the stages of concern. Hall and Hord (2001) coined the idea of an "innovation configuration map" to represent a "typical" range of steps through the change process. This continuum provides staff with a clear picture of what the

6.1

Excerpt from Action Plan
Time line: Winter-Spring

	Goal: Complete curriculum maps for all subject areas		
Date	**Action to be taken**	**Person(s) responsible**	**Evidence that action has been taken**
1/15	Teachers will have been assigned to subject-area teams to develop a draft-curriculum map. The map will include the understandings, essential questions, key knowledge and skills, and core assessments.	• Ann	A memo sent to staff delineating the team assignments
2/15	Develop a continuum to measure the quality of the use of the subject-area maps. Will be distributed to all staff for use in formative self-assessment and for summative assessment by the principal at the end of each team's work.	• Change facilitator team	Distribution of curriculum map continuum along with faculty meeting agenda where the continuum will be presented and the process for summative assessment will be explained
2/28	Those teachers assigned to the subject-area teams for language arts and science will participate in an Understanding by Design training that teaches the principles of backward planning as tailored to the school's curriculum mapping process.	• Tom • Change facilitator team	Evaluation forms by all teachers attending the training session
2/28	Long-term training schedule for other subject-area teams for training sessions with Tom (includes summer and next school year).	• Tom • Change facilitator team	Long-term training schedule

6.1 *(continued)*
Excerpt from Action Plan
Time line: Winter-Spring

	Goal: Complete curriculum maps for all subject areas		
Date	**Action to be taken**	**Person(s) responsible**	**Evidence that action has been taken**
3/15	Each team will be allotted a sum of money to cover work on the maps. The team can allocate those funds to pay for supplemental curriculum development time, hire substitutes for release time during the school day, and/or purchase food for dinner meetings. Each team will develop a schedule for team meetings necessary to complete the work.	• Joan and subject-area teams	A memo to each team outlining the budget, the guidelines for approved expenses, and forms for submitting their budget proposals
3/30	Each member of the change facilitator team will have a schedule of the meetings and assignments to make sure that the teams get the feedback and guidance they need in a timely fashion.	• Ann	List of meetings and identification of the member of the change facilitator team assigned to each meeting

innovation should look like over time as staff members move from novice to sophisticated user of the innovation. What typically happens when these pictures are not available is that staff members are left to their own to make assumptions about what the indicators of success might be and when they are "done" with the change process. Most often these assumptions lead to significant misconceptions about the perceived practice, actual practice, and desired practice. For instance, if the innovation is to bring inquiry-based education into the classroom:

> A teacher with a well-articulated schema for project-based science might observe a classroom where students are engaged in multiple animated conversations around computers or desks covered with laboratory notebooks, printouts, and resource materials, and perceive it as an engaging inquiry science experience. Another teacher might perceive it as a chaotic classroom in need of better management. Similarly, different teachers may receive the same "policy message" and interpret an idea such as "inquiry" in very different ways. (Spillane, Reiser, & Reimer, 2002, pp. 396–397)

The continuum fosters a culture of collective autonomy because it builds consensus among all staff about what the innovation looks like when it is successfully implemented (Hall and Hord 2001).

Figures 6.2 and 6.3 are two examples of continuums showing the stages of curriculum alignment with state standards.

To produce "visual" descriptions that are both clear and broadly applicable, individuals must be selected who know what the innovation will look like at various points on the continuum. These participants will likely include the change facilitator team as well as additional staff or consultant(s) who have a high level of expertise and experience with the innovation. This writing team will need to allocate substantial time for this endeavor to allow sufficient time to think aloud about what "success" looks like and how to articulate that conception in a way that is faithful to the innovation, mindful of the shared vision, and accessible to all staff. Based on experience, to achieve this level of clarity, coherence, and accuracy requires several drafts, time between writing sessions to gain some distance from the language, and feedback and guidance from representative members of the staff who will be using the continuum once it is completed. Without this foundation, each point on the continuum will likely be a mix of wild guesses and philosophies.

Once the continuum is developed, staff will need training to learn how this measurement tool can be used as a way to gauge their own progress as well as identify what support they might need in order to achieve the next level of implementation. The change facilitator team also can use the tool as a means to track staff proficiency and discern general patterns about strengths and areas of concern in the implementation of the staff development plan. This data collection allows leaders to make informed judgments about the

6.2

Continuum on Alignment of Curriculum with State Content Standards
(Through the Lens of Teacher Instruction)

Nonexistent	Beginning	Emerging	Prominent
Instruction is driven by a need to "cover the text" or the content "we have always taught." There is no implicit or explicit reference to state or district standards. Lecture dominates and focuses on the content knowledge and skills within the unit, with, at best, rare references to other units completed earlier or yet to come, and equally rare references to concepts within the discipline.	Instruction is driven by a need to "cover" the state or district content standards. Lecture and the use of worksheets dominate and focus on the teaching or practice of discrete skills and content. References are rarely made to units completed earlier or yet to come. The concepts of a discipline are discretely taught with no reference to their relation to the content knowledge and skills within the unit.	Instruction is driven by a need to "uncover" how the content knowledge and skills within a unit are related to the concepts that can be used to organize the unit's content. The content and skills are derived directly from the state or district standards. Rarely if ever are the concepts or content of a unit seen as a logical extension of the earlier units, or a precursor of those that will follow. Questions become the focus of instruction as the students are challenged to organize the content in ways that will help them recall it.	Instruction is driven by a need to "uncover" major concepts that provide the focus of the course, the program, and the discipline. Typically, the content knowledge and skills in the state or district standards are taught in a manner that encourages the development of the concepts or a conscious revisiting of them so that students' understanding of the concepts becomes more sophisticated. Instruction largely relies on a variety of questioning strategies, with the focus of the unit being established through the repeated use of "essential questions."

6.3

Continuum on Alignment of Curriculum with State Content Standards (Through the Lens of Student Performance)

Nonexistent	Beginning	Emerging	Prominent
Students show through their discussion and in their products uncertainty about what is important in and why it is important. A frequent comment is "Why do I have to know this? I'm never going to use it." Equally common are such comments as "Will it be on the test?" "How many pages do you want?" and "I don't care; just tell me what you want." Student performance typically shows a lack of effort.	Students show through discussion and in their products a retention of the discrete content knowledge and an accurate but not always appropriate application of technical skills in the state or district content standards. They see all knowledge and skills as unrelated and equally important, and they memorize material as the means to pass the state or district high-stakes tests.	Students show through discussion and in their products a mastery of the discrete knowledge and skills in the state or district content standards, and how the knowledge and skills interrelate conceptually within units. They can use a concept to explain knowledge or the appropriate use of skills. But they recognize the real value of a concept as a framework on which to hang the content so that they can remember it for state or district high-stakes assessments.	Students show through discussion and in their products a consistent struggle to make connections among the discrete knowledge and skills in a course. In doing so, they are discovering the conceptual framework of the discipline and the sense this framework gives to the knowledge and skills being studied. They see the concepts within this framework as being important to their success in processing information and solving complex problems—in sum, addressing the challenges of a rich, productive life.

functionality of the original action plan and to make appropriate modifications to optimize the effectiveness of the means (staff development) in helping to achieve the desired end (shared vision).

In addition to the articulation of a continuum of what the innovation looks like at various phases of implementation, the second key concept that influences the initial and ongoing development of an action plan is the predictable stages of concern experienced during the change process. Although many educators readily acknowledge that learning and the associated change are emotional experiences, it is with much hesitation that they offer suggestions on how to handle staff responses. Scenarios ranging from passive resistance to outright defiance haunt leaders in charge of implementation, reminiscent of conversations and reflections found in the opening three chapters. Even though every system is unique, there is a high degree of predictability in the types of concerns that are raised throughout the implementation of an innovation. As the following figure (Figure 6.4) illustrates, implementing a change follows what Glickman (1993) describes as "a rather commonsensical [and predictable] three-phase sequence" (p. 75).

1. **The change must be explained and then modeled to staff.** (Hall and Hord, Stages 1 and 2)—When teachers first go through the process of new learning, they are concerned with what the benefits of the innovation will be, how other teachers (and systems) have done it, and how it will change established practices. They need to know what the innovation looks like and how it may make their teaching life better. It has to be explained and modeled for them.

2. **Opportunities must be given for "role playing, applied practice, and feedback" by a knowledgeable and nonjudgmental coach.** (Hall and Hord, Stage 3)—As teachers face the experience of actually using the new practice, they are concerned with how to make it work. With a familiar practice, they have learned how to implement it comfortably and have resolved questions about resources, appropriate use, effective teacher behaviors for implementation, and the amount of energy to expend on it. Now they face discomfort and a set of issues around making the new practice work. They also face the question of gain and loss: "What am I gaining when it would be far more

6.4

Stages of Concern in the Change Process

Hall and Hord		Glickman
I M P A C T	**Stage 6: Refocusing** Change is collaborative as I work with others to focus on adaptation or alternatives to the innovation to achieve even better student results.	**Refinement** How can I take this change to a higher level of expertise in my classroom? How am I working with colleagues to brainstorm desirable modifications, to tie it more directly to the school's overall direction? Concentration is on exploring, troubleshooting, brainstorming, and problem solving.
	Stage 5: Collaboration Change becomes collaborative as I think about how to coordinate implementation with colleagues to ensure even better student results.	
	Stage 4: Consequence The focus has shifted from how the change affects me to how it affects students.	
T A S K	**Stage 3: Management** The focus is on organizing resources, effort, and energy so that the innovation is managed efficiently.	**Integration** How does this work? How should I use it with students? Concentration is on exploration, implementation, and feedback.
S E L F	**Stage 2: Personal** The focus is on the effect of the innovation on me. I have concerns about my role in the process, whether I can do it, and how it will affect my existing status with stakeholders and my relationships with colleagues.	**Orientation** Why do I need to learn this? How will it help my students? How will it make my life better? Concentration is on getting clearer on what the initiative is, what new skills and knowledge will need to be learned, and how it will affect current practice.
	Stage 1: Informational I'm generally aware of the innovation and interested in learning more, but haven't yet thought about its impact on me and my work in the classroom.	
	Stage 0: Awareness I have little or no concern or involvement.	

Source: Adapted from *Implementing Change: Patterns, Principles, and Potholes* (pp. 56–79), by G. E. Hall & S. M. Hord, 2001, Boston: Allyn & Bacon; and *Renewing America's Schools* (pp. 76–79), by C. Glickman, 1993, San Francisco: Jossey-Bass.

comfortable to keep doing what I have already done?" To prevent the teacher from abandoning the innovation and simply reverting to the old practice, knowledgeable and nonjudgmental coaching involving "role playing, applied practice, and feedback" (Glickman, 1993, p. 77) is needed.

3. **Time must be provided for discussing the change, brainstorming desirable modifications, and revising the use of the new approach.** (Hall and Hord, Stages 4 through 6)—At the impact stage, staff members raise questions about how they can coordinate their efforts and how they can modify the innovation to increase student achievement even more, a hallmark of collective autonomy.

   It is possible, however, that staff moves to this stage too early in the change process, with negative (rather than positive) repercussions. This occurs when teachers decide, "This innovation is not working for me, my students, and probably not for my colleagues either." Therefore, they either soften or abandon the innovation and refocus on what is familiar, on what has "worked" in the past.

Figure 6.5 presents examples of the types of teacher concerns that accompany any change effort. By expressing such concerns, teachers are investing in continuous improvement. Their concerns are legitimate and require effective but different change facilitation to ensure that staff development leads to progress toward the shared vision. Effective change facilitation is necessary for achieving collective autonomy, for if teachers do not see the system supporting them, they will not, in turn, support systemic efforts. "What's in it for me if the system is not working for me?" becomes the pitfall preventing collective autonomy.

It is important to note that the examples merely illustrate some of the concerns and issues that may arise during the change process; many more examples can be imagined. The examples in the figure, however, make the case for observing the following guidelines:

➤ Preplan for predictable staff concerns.
➤ Provide staff with necessary training, coaching, and resources.

6.5

Examples of Staff Concerns at Various Stages of the Change Process

Stages of Concern	Staff Concerns Making sense of the innovations
Stage 6: Refocusing Change is collaborative as I work with others to focus on adaptation or alternatives to the innovation to achieve even better student results.	"As we talk more and more about the weaknesses in student achievement, we're finding that the school really has two populations: those who are new to the school or district and score low on all measures of achievement and those who have been around for a while and score high. It's really a bipolar distribution. We need to focus on how to better integrate the low-achieving students into the system without falling back on a simplistic 'more time on task' answer. We need to look at the research around a kind of IEP for low-achieving students and redirect more resources to provide the additional support they need. We might look at reassigning staff not on the simple formula of class size but on a mix of class size and magnitude of need in the class population."
Stage 5: Collaboration Change becomes collaborative as I think about how to coordinate with colleagues in implementation to ensure even better students results.	"As I talked with my colleagues, it became clearer to us that, if we modify the unit on the American Revolution by focusing on a problem-based assessment piece, we might get better results."
Stage 4: Consequence The focus has shifted from how the change affects me to how it affects students.	"I need to talk with the other teachers at this grade level who are teaching the same unit and share with them our successes and failures. I think we can learn from one another if we coordinate our efforts."

6.5 *(continued)*

Examples of Staff Concerns at Various Stages of the Change Process

Stages of Concern	Staff Concerns Making sense of the innovations
Stage 3: Management The focus is on organizing resources, effort, and energy so that the innovation is managed efficiently.	"I'm giving it a try, but I need new resources. Can you get me the new science materials and then help me plan how to integrate them into my classes? What about team-teaching with me, or, maybe better, teach a class of mine so I can see how the new approach can be successful with the new resources?"
Stage 2: Personal The focus is on the effect of the innovation on me. I have concerns about my role in the process, whether I can do it, and how it will affect my existing status with stakeholders and my relationships with colleagues.	"This approach is so complicated, I'm not sure that it won't kill me in the short run! I'm not even sure that, if I do survive, I can do it well enough."
Stage 1: Informational I'm generally aware of the innovation and interested in learning more, but haven't yet thought about its impact on me and my work in the classroom.	"OK, I see that curriculum mapping linked to Understanding By Design might be a better way of getting our act together, but I can't be sure until I learn more. I'm ready to listen."
Stage 0: Awareness I have little or no concern or involvement.	"What is curriculum mapping and Understanding by Design? How is it similar to and how is it different from what we're already doing? I have so much on my plate right now, and I need to be real clear on what's new and what's old so that I can get this done as quickly as possible."

Source: Stages of Concern are adapted from *Implementing Change: Patterns, Principles, and Potholes* (pp. 56–79), by G. E. Hall & S. M. Hord, 2001, Boston: Allyn & Bacon.

➤ Support teachers as they collaborate; demonstrate concretely that you value their collaborative intentions and efforts.

➤ Modify the plans as teacher comments or behaviors indicate that they collectively or individually need differentiated support or training.

Although it is not possible to anticipate all staff concerns in the planning process, the change facilitator team can brainstorm predictable concerns and plan accordingly. "I don't even have a copy of the new state standards and I hear there are too many" is a predictable informational concern in the curriculum mapping process (Stage 1), but it can also be a predictable personal concern (Stage 2) for the staff members who feel overwhelmed by these standards and do not know how to cope. By providing necessary information through a series of planned actions, the facilitator team can meet both the informational concern and the related personal concern for most of the staff. A change facilitator team can also anticipate the task concerns (Stage 3), such as "How do I incorporate state standards into my unit plans and actual teaching?" and "How do I know that I'm doing my job and getting students ready for state assessments?" Because task concerns relate directly to teacher competence, failure to predict such concerns may doom the innovation when teachers are expected to put it into practice. Impact concerns (Stages 4 through 6) are also predictable, particularly as the facilitator team sees teachers progress with the innovation. The team has to anticipate that teachers will want opportunities to work with colleagues on ways to modify the innovation for enhanced student learning and achievement.

As the change facilitator team leads staff through these predictable, but serious concerns, they must: "Listen carefully but maintain a sharp focus on the end" (Mauer, 1996, p. 54, as cited in Fullan, 2001, p. 75). Educators must be granted the time, space, and support to "uncover" what the innovations look like, how they function, and why they are valuable in our classrooms, with these students, in this subject area. At the same time, staff members must be consistently brought back to the shared vision of the work so that they come to trust that this change is a collective endeavor; individual success is a necessary but not sufficient measurement about whether the staff development plan has closed the gap between what the system aspires to become and current performance levels.

Before wrapping up the conversation and analysis on action planning, it is important to reflect on a subtle, but powerful emotion that underlies the implementation of any innovation: grief over the loss of the familiar. This emotion is likely to arise regardless of the effectiveness of the threatened habitual practice. The attachment to past practice is based on interactions with other people, the self-esteem and self-fulfillment derived from the classroom and school, and the investment in values that the past practice represents (Van den Berg 2002).

Staff Conversation #10

It's five minutes before the beginning of classes, and Joan is walking through the halls checking in with teachers. This check-in has become a new part of her morning routine because she finds that the information gained from these casual and brief encounters is as, if not more, helpful to thinking about the change process as any formal meeting on the subject. She sees Rob toward the end of the corridor and quickens her pace so she can catch him before the bell rings. Joan has been concerned about him lately; he has really dropped out of the conversations this year, and she does not know why.

Joan: Morning, Rob! Just wanted to know if I can drop into your classroom sometime today. Always enjoy watching how you engage students in important work.

Rob: Not sure that today is a good day to do that, but you can come anyway.

Joan: Would tomorrow be better?

Rob: It depends on what you're looking for. I don't think that I'm the poster child of this staff development work right now.

Joan: Every teacher in this building is a work in progress. Just wanted to see how you're working to make sense of this in the classroom. Come on, Rob. You were doing this kind of work even before we began this change process.

Rob: That's what I thought, too, but in my efforts to get clearer about what I expect kids to know and be able to do, I've lost my passion for the content in the first place. This work is killing me.

Joan: I don't think I understand what you mean exactly. I really want to understand.

Rob: I used to conceptualize what I teach based on the important issues and questions at the heart of the unit. Now because of the curriculum mapping work, I've been trying to explicitly define the "content" of what I do and think through the reasoning behind that approach. This push to articulate the "nuts and bolts" of the curriculum is killing why I love to teach.

Joan: So, what I'm hearing is that your focus on the content standards, knowledge, and skills is competing with your passion for the "big ideas." It sounds as if we have to think about how you can complete the curriculum maps but perhaps through a different entry point. No one ever said that there was just one way to complete this process. It's also likely that you're not the only one with this struggle. [*Becoming increasingly uncomfortable with the public venue of such a personal discussion, Joan suggests moving the conversation to a more appropriate time and place.*] We can talk more about this later. Why don't you come down to my office after school today? [*One of the students, overhearing Joan's last statement as he's entering the classroom, says, "Oooooh. Mr. Kalmanson is in trouble! He has to go to the principal's office."*]

Rob: [*More to himself than to Joan*] I was just thinking the same thing. When exactly did I become "the teacher who needs help"?

Analysis of Staff Conversation #10

Because the implementation of an innovation involves change, it also involves loss: "loss of ease with comfortable practices. Inevitably, accepting something new often means letting go of something old" (Brown & Moffett, 1999, p. 52). Although this emotional unrest is unsettling, it is unavoidable. Van den Berg's extensive review of research on teacher concerns (2002) cites teachers' deep attachment to their work. "The implementation of educational developments always gives rise to internal turmoil and is always influenced by the already existing patterns of culture, power, and control" (p. 583).

As teachers make changes that require new knowledge and new skills, they confront the feeling of loss not only in confidence but also in technical competence in doing what is at the core of their job. Fullan (2001) coined the phrase "implementation dip" to describe this temporary loss of competence, an unavoidable feature of "all innovations worth their salt"(p. 40-41). To lead staff through this unsettling time requires sensitive and skilled coaching as well as patience in demanding to see results (both in measuring staff performance and the effectiveness of the staff development plan).

Just because the "implementation dip" is well documented in change literature does not mean that it is common knowledge for staff (or, even if it becomes common knowledge, that the emotions associated with it are any less unsettling).

Providing support for a teacher who is grieving looks (and sounds) very different from providing direction for a teacher who is "blocking" the process for other reasons. Rob's last remark in his conversation with Joan suggests that the source of his discomfort stems from becoming "the teacher who needs help." Although this comment is directed as much to himself as to Joan, her response to Rob's concern is crucial to his continued participation in the change process.

Summing Up and Looking Ahead

The notion that "change is a process, not an event" is widely embraced by both researchers and practitioners alike (Fullan 2001, p. 40; Hall and Hord 2001, p. 4). However, the pressure on leaders to produce immediate results tempt many to find an "off-the-shelf" solution or follow a prescribed series of action planning steps. This chapter once again reinforces the unavoidable complexity of building collective autonomy and implementing an innovation, but also provides some key tools to develop and revise a plan in a way that honors concerns and helps staff work through them. While all members of the staff play a significant role in the implementation of any innovation, it is important to underscore that the planning effort remains the responsibility of the change facilitator team. It is the team's job to devise the plan, to implement the plan, and then to revisit the plan regularly to make sure it is still on target. For a more contextualized approach to action planning, see Appendix B. That role is distinctly different from the work of the teachers. Their work is to plan lessons and units, to implement them, to assess achievement, and to refine lessons and units based on assessment data, and finally, to build the

➤

interpersonal relations necessary to ensure both horizontal and vertical program coherence (Schmoker, 2003; Fullan, 2001).

Joan's next step: She must work to ensure that the conditions for collective accountability are in place. These conditions are embedded in a competent system.

The staff's next step: They must endorse and embrace collective accountability as being essential to continuous improvement and a competent system.

The reader's next step: With your school and your district in mind, consider the following questions:

➤ What is the action plan for your innovation? Does it account for the ripple that is part of any complex change effort? How do you plan for the ripple effects without becoming distracted from your purpose?

➤ What are the observable indicators we can use to measure success of implementation? Who decides? Who evaluates? Are these evaluations intended to audit individual or collective performance levels? Both?

➤ What are the predictable concerns that staff is likely to face working with these innovations? How do we build those concerns into the design of the action plan?

➤ Are some concerns more legitimate than others? Are some levels of resistance more legitimate than others? How do we differentiate for ourselves? How do we help others to differentiate?

WELCOMING ACCOUNTABILITY ON THE ROAD TO SUCCESS

Essential Question:

Who's accountable and for what?

Operating Principle

– A competent system proves itself when everyone within the system performs better as a result of the collective endeavors and accepts accountability for that improvement.

Chapter Overview

This chapter addresses the sixth and final step in the continuous improvement effort: Embrace collective autonomy as the only way to close the gaps between the current reality and the shared vision, and embrace collective accountability in establishing responsibility for closing the gaps. Collective accountability must extend from the formal leadership to leaders who emerge during the change process to all staff members. They must all see themselves as collectively and individually responsible for building a competent system, fulfilling the shared vision, and achieving the desired results. They must all commit to being accountable for enhanced learning and achievement for all students.

This step requires nothing short of a resocialization of staff and a solidification of trust. Staff members must do more than embrace the innovations as a way to broaden their repertoire; they must change how they function in the classroom. They must collectively and individually assume responsibility for both process and results.

This chapter illuminates the conditions necessary for collective accountability: shared leadership and teaching as a distributed quality. At the end of this final chapter, the fictional school has "become" a competent system as stakeholders continue to collect and analyze data to determine gaps between the shared vision and the reality so that they can further improve academic achievement and move closer to equity for all. "Here goodness not only reflects the current workings of the institution but also how far it has come and where it is headed" (Lightfoot, 1983, p. 24). Staff members, and in this chapter most notably the superintendent, Henry, recognize that this effort to improve student achievement is a collective one in which every member of the school community has a part to play and accountability for playing that role successfully.

Principal Reflection #6

As the students' school day ends, Joan stands in the center of the lobby anticipating the exchanges she will have with the students as they leave. She smiles as she sees the first bus pull in front of the school and hears the bell signaling the end of the day.

Joan can be found in the lobby every morning and every afternoon. She came to these habits not out of a sense of wanting to look like a principal but, instead, out of a genuine need to see the school in all of its complexity. As she seamlessly transitions from her role as traffic cop to well-wisher to authority figure to instructional leader, she is inspired by the possibilities that each day and each year bring to the school community. Her thoughts purposely focus on this last role: instructional leader. She surveys the diversity of the student body and contemplates the ranges in background, abilities, interests, and styles. She thinks of the unique experiences that characterize the learning environment of each classroom and the common curricular threads that now link them all together. Out of this rich context, powerful relationships emerge as teachers and students collaborate to reach high, clearly defined achievement standards. In the midst of these deep thoughts, Joan notices that the framed statement of core beliefs hung on the wall next to the main entrance is slightly crooked. As she straightens it, she proudly scans the words she already knows by heart: "Our school community is dedicated to excellence. It is an excellence defined by the commitment of all to achieve at the highest level and to ensure equity of access and standards in all aspects of the school community." Balancing the demands of a pursuit of high achievement and equity has proven to be a worthy but difficult endeavor to uphold for all members of the school community. At what point does the emphasis on equity threaten standards? At what point does the emphasis on high standards become unfair to some students and some teachers? How do we ensure that all teachers remain individually empowered as they exercise collective effort? How do we empower all students to take charge of their learning and still meet society's expectations?

Joan's deep thoughts are once again interrupted, this time by the mad dash of a student through the main lobby, just missing the last bus as it pulls out of the parking lot. As Joan walks the student into the main office so that her secretary can contact the boy's parent, she asks him how his science fair project is going. The student responds: "It's awesome how even the smallest creatures have homes and food and jobs and families. I am uncovering things about ants that make me really see them in a whole new light! I understand insects in a whole new way."

Maria happens to walk by Joan right at that moment and flashes a smile. "Great to see so many students involved in discovery, huh?" says Maria.

"More than you know," Joan sincerely replies.

Staff Conversation #11

Joan heads for the conference room to meet with Ann and Susan. The change facilitator team meetings have become regular fixtures since the work began more than two years ago. They dedicate at least an hour a week to talk through staff concerns that have arisen, to monitor progress, and to revisit and revise the action plan as appropriate. Because the school year is almost over, the three of them plan to meet for several hours to reflect on the accomplishments and issues that have unfolded during the year and then join Ed for dinner to review their findings together. Their afternoon conversation covers a wide range of topics. Among them is the fact that three staff members are leaving the school: one early retirement, one transfer, and one resignation. All three individuals are leaving because it has become increasingly apparent that their core beliefs are incompatible with those of the school. Although this attrition is to be expected, it is still painful to lose people along the way. The change facilitator team also is concerned about the message it sends to staff; on the one hand, it is clear that all staff are held accountable to achieve desired results, but on the other hand, it is clear that the administrators are very much in control of the system. The team will continue to brainstorm ways to listen to resisters and learn from them, but they remain adamant that no individual will compromise the collective autonomy of the system.

Ann: One of us may finally identify the solution to attrition, but that will be because of expertise, interest, style, or formal authority, not because it is a problem one of us owns. This place is not a one-person band. I now know that, for sure.

Susan: We have become much sharper in identifying needs, sharing this information, testing for patterns in needs, and then responding to individual, subgroup, and full-group needs more promptly and more sensitively.

Joan: I think it also has been key that we've kept the focus on the shared vision. We've been authoritative but we depersonalized that authoritativeness by ensuring that origin and responsibility by staff as a whole are always as clear as the vision itself. Staff members who've been vigorous in articulating their concerns have really caused us to reexamine plans for closing the gap and the nature of the change process itself. I think we've become more sophisticated in the support we provide.

Ann: It's a good mix of the authority required by our collective moral commitment to the vision and the sensitivity of a collegial coach. Let me develop a list of exactly what it is we learned. Let me try to put the lessons in terms of guiding principles for our future work.

The change facilitator team then moves on to identifying a list of issues that have emerged as essential to the next phase of the staff development work.

➤ Using analysis of current research to address the bipolar distribution of assessment results. ("Bipolar" referring to the distribution's indication that the school really has two populations: those who are new to the school or district and score low on all measures of achievement, and those who have been around for a while and score high.)
➤ Coaching teachers as they continue their work on innovations, especially in writing understandings and assessments.
➤ Building the number of core assessments.
➤ Refining the existing schoolwide rubrics and increasing the scope of the traits for which there are rubrics.
➤ Building a cadre of parents who are willing to collaborate with teacher teams to build problem-based learning units that truly mirror the ways adults use the knowledge and skills we teach.
➤ Providing time for discussions of common problems, collaborative planning, examining student work, and refining curriculum maps to ensure coherence across grades.
➤ Identifying emerging teacher leaders.
➤ Formally celebrating successes and successful collective behaviors.

As the discussion of these points unfolds, the three agree to divide the tasks, set out an action plan for each, and then meet again to review, refine, and integrate the plans for the next year. Ann assumes leadership responsibility for developing the plans for

➤ Coaching the teachers in language arts and science, and
➤ Revisiting and revising the maps.

Susan assumes leadership responsibility for developing the plans for

➤ Analyzing the bipolar distribution of assessment results, and
➤ Researching materials on effective practices with the underachieving student.

Joan assumes leadership responsibility for developing the plans for

➤ Providing time for more substantive discussions of common problems, collaborative planning, and refining the curriculum maps to better ensure coherent learning experiences in science and language arts; and

➤ Formally celebrating successes and successful collective behaviors.

The team decides to ask Maria and Rob to lead the effort at building core assessments and designing rubrics because of their interest in the issue from the beginning of the journey and their emerging leadership in the development of the initial assessments and rubrics. Joan agrees to meet with Maria and Rob and help them construct an action plan for this phase of the work. The issue regarding parent involvement is placed on hold until next year's work begins to unfold. Ann suggests that Miguel might be a good leader for the future effort with parents.

After reviewing their findings with Ed over dinner, he gives them feedback on their growth as a team.

Ed: [Smiling broadly] Well, you've certainly identified your interests and areas of expertise. Ann, you continue to be a teacher leader, always in the trenches working with the teachers and focusing on learning. Susan, you really have emerged as a teacher leader too; you ensure that the problems are validly analyzed and that the solutions have intellectual integrity and focus on closing the gaps. Joan, you've grown to become a powerful systems thinker, focusing on the patterns of elements and relationships that define the school and keeping them in balance. I'm so impressed with how well you work together as a team, in terms of expertise, interest, and authority.

Analysis of Staff Conversation #11

As Ann commented in the conversation at the beginning of the chapter, leadership is shared. It arises from multiple sources: expertise, interest, style, or formal authority. When accountability is collective, every staff member can become a leader. Leadership is assigned based on who is the most qualified to oversee the particular effort.

> Shared leadership recognizes the concepts of shared fate and shared accountability. . . . It requires that leaders know each other and that all members of the leader-follower team have a reasonable assessment of the strengths, weaknesses, and tendencies of each of their peers. . . . As a group the shared decision-making team is less like an orchestra, where the conductor is always in charge, and more like a jazz band, where leadership is passed around among the players depending on what the music demands at the moment and who feels most moved by the spirit to express that music. (Schlechty, 2001, p.178)

The concept of shared leadership strengthens collective accountability for it envisions that all members of the school community can become leaders in achieving the desired results. Leadership becomes a distributed property.

This is where leadership and teaching as distributed qualities come together. Shared leadership must guide and support teachers through the change process; teachers must have the opportunity to learn so that they can, in turn, improve student performance. Leaders must provide teachers access to one another to work through problems together and to learn from one another's solutions. In this setting every teacher becomes a teacher leader. "In the panoply of rewards and sanctions that attach to accountability systems, the most powerful incentives reside in the face-to-face relationships among people in organizations, not in external systems" (Elmore, as cited in Fullan, 2001, p. 131). Further, where leadership is shared, leaders avoid sorting staff along lines of who is leading, who is following, and who has yet to move. Such labeling of "pioneers" and "settlers" generally undermines collective accountability for achieving the desired results. Although attention to individual staff members is relevant and necessary, such attention should be done to target resources and support as appropriate so that the gaps can be closed between the shared vision and current performance levels.

Administrator Conversation #5

As Joan enters Henry's office, she is both excited and nervous. She is here for the annual evaluation of her performance as a principal. The school is well along in the change effort but still has a way to go. Several of the staff members who are furthest along have begun to refocus on a gap between practice and belief that had been identified earlier but hadn't been dealt with—issues around the beliefs associated with equity. She knows that Henry will be pleased that average scores are up, but she and the staff already have begun to think about who that "average" represents. Why have the scores in the lowest quartile remained static? The bipolar distribution of achievement has recently assumed top priority for her staff. After analyzing the data that showed the significance of the gap between the lowest quartile of students and the rest of the students, staff members have been brainstorming how to make substantial changes quickly. They have had some preliminary conversations about lowering the class size in targeted areas. Although this change will raise class sizes for most of the teachers in the school, they believe it is worth the sacrifice so that they can more effectively reach out to students who need individualized attention. Two of Joan's most capable teachers have also volunteered to be reassigned to teach these students either as part of their daily schedule or as an after-school program. Joan is clear that her objective in the meeting she is about to have with Henry is to make sure they are on the same page: that the job to raise student achievement is far from done. Armed with recently collected data (from both external and internal assessments) and the revised action plan, Joan enters the meeting. After exchanging customary pleasantries, they get down to the business at hand. Joan hands Henry the latest data on student achievement.

Joan: Henry, as you can see, you have this year's scores on the state test as well as the initial scores from core assessments we developed for two subject areas, assessments designed to measure achievement at two-year intervals. Although we have no comparative data for the locally developed assessments, we do for the state tests. You can see that average achievement is going up, but the results for the lowest-scoring group remain very weak. We're beginning to talk about why this bipolar distribution is happening, and, in fact, becoming more extreme. We have some tentative hypotheses, but we don't have confidence in any of them yet. We're researching who these students are and looking for academic variables that define them as a group and that differentiate them from the higher-achieving students. That work remains to be finished. Although we don't have comparative data on local assessments, we think the students are doing better on the state tests than they are on our locally designed ones. This hasn't been a surprise because we believe the local tests more validly measure understanding than the state tests do. Frankly, we think the local tests are more rigorous. We're looking for patterns to see if we find areas where most students are having difficulty regardless of how they scored on the state tests. When we find them, we're then looking to see if the assessments are faulty—for instance, unclear—or if there's a gap in our instruction that we need to close. This work, too, needs to be finished. What's most exciting is that data have become less threatening to staff members. They're in control of it. The consultant, Tom, has helped staff learn how to read numbers, but, finally, the teachers have taken control of the analysis. We'll be back with a more thorough analysis by the start of next year. Maybe you'll want to share the results with the board and the public before next year's state test results are reported.

Henry: How did you arrive at the distribution of scores you report on the local assessments? Who scored them? On what basis?

Joan: Our teachers scored them using common rubrics.

Henry: Did you test for inter-rater reliability among scores by different teachers?

Joan: Oh, yes. Tom warned us that we would have to. We achieved an inter-rater reliability of about 92 percent. The literature on testing says that's pretty good.

Henry: It is. I'm impressed. I also am pleased with the increase in average scores on the state tests, but, like you, I'm puzzled by the bipolar distribution. I'm interested in what you'll uncover. I'm also going to be looking at whether or not your initial findings about the distribution are applicable to other schools in the district.

Joan: If you find that our results indeed have systemwide implications, I'd be happy to share with other principals the strategies that our staff members are developing to close the gap. I wouldn't presume that what works in our school will work everywhere, but I do think the operating principles that shape and reshape our work will have relevance.

Henry: I used to be concerned that you would isolate your system from the district system. But, instead, you've evolved into a powerful leader on both fronts. Your colleagues, all of us, listen carefully to what you say. Frankly, we couldn't do without you.

Joan: Well, you don't have to worry about that. At the same time, I do think it is worth noting that, if I'm doing my job well, this change effort should be more than the product of my efforts. Doesn't a good leader share leadership while still acknowledging differences in formal authority? Doesn't a good leader expect others to exercise leadership when responsibility and expertise suggest it? If you really want to get a clear picture of the work being done in the building to raise student achievement across the board, you should come and see it for yourself: not only the substance of what the staff is saying about closing the gap but the extent to which they've embraced collective autonomy and collective accountability. They really believe that we're in this together: that the work in every classroom is the work of the school. There's no way for me to put it into words, and, believe me, I've tried on more than one occasion to show what actually is happening.

Henry: You know, I think I will come and see for myself.

He and Joan finish the remainder of her evaluation conference. As he walks Joan out of the office, he stops at his secretary's desk and asks her to coordinate a time with Joan for him to come to the school. He tells both Joan and the secretary that the duration and structure of the visit will be determined by Joan.

Principal Reflection #7

As is typical, Joan's reflection continues long after her meeting with Henry is over. Driving back to her school, she reflects on how far both she and her staff have come in the last few years. It has been hard work, resulting in some bumps and bruises along the way, but the sacrifice has been well worth it: the shared vision has become a fixture in the system. Her biggest concern these days is about the level of collaboration with key stakeholders who work outside the walls of the school, especially parents who have yet to see the powerful effect of collective accountability on the achievement of either their own children or the student body as a whole. Given this lack of understanding, they could not be expected to join the staff in conversations that grew from this sense of collective accountability. Joan's concern stems not only from parents' exclusive focus on their own children but also from staff members who still feel guarded at the prospect of parents' participation in what were formerly private professional conversations. A comment one of her staff members made last year at a faculty meeting comes to mind: "Do you know any other business where the customers think they know better than the professionals?" Did distrust, good sense, or insecurity prompt this remark? As Joan puzzles over the answer to the question, it becomes clear that this issue demands immediate attention; but she still needs to gain more clarity on what the desired results would be and whom to include in that conversation. She also wonders if Miguel has the expertise to actively engage parents in the work of the school.

Staff Conversation #12 and Reflection

A week after Joan's evaluation meeting with Henry, the two of them are walking to a meeting with staff members who are working to translate research into practice on how to increase the performance of the lowest quartile of students. Joan motions for Henry to come into Rob's classroom for a minute. Rob is talking with his students about the core assessments that they will be taking next week.

Henry is instantly struck by the lack of tension in the room. Why aren't the students more anxious? He knows that Rob is taking on a leadership role in the building to create the core assessments and scoring rubrics, but are those assessments and rubrics evaluating the right things? Too often, in Henry's experience, teachers have demonstrated to him that who the student is colors how they evaluate that student's achievement. The only saving grace of this subjective evaluation is that the same teachers strive to do this in the best interest of students. In his mind, this tendency raises serious questions about teachers' ability to function as reliable assessors of student achievement. He knows that some staff members in the district think he relies far too much on state test scores. But, from his perspective, these have proven to be the only set of numbers that are trustworthy because they are in alignment with accepted standards about what all students should know and be able to do.

The bell rings, signaling the end of the school day, which means that Joan is off to the school lobby. In the few minutes before Henry has to go to the meeting, he decides to press Rob on the issue of the rigor of the core assessments and their scoring.

Henry: Rob, I noticed on the results from the mid-year core assessments that students' performance levels are lower than they are on state assessments. Do you have any insights into why that might be the case?

Rob: Sure. What we're assessing is understanding. What the state assesses is mostly knowledge and skill.

Henry: But how can you isolate understanding without focusing on knowledge and skill?

Rob: *[As Rob explains to Henry what understanding is and how it functions, he is very aware of what a long two years it has been for him—long in every sense of the word. He has made such progress in his thinking about quality teaching and learning. At the same time, he feels less sure of his uniqueness as an educator. He reflects on his evolution.]* I used to really see myself as working in spite of the system. In my mind I was a beacon of hope for kids who had been bored or disenfranchised in other classrooms. In my classroom they were valued not only for what they think but also what they have the potential to become, regardless of past performance. Now, instead of feeling like I was at the forefront of educational reform, I have a more realistic picture of myself. My way of thinking about my own practices on a continuum of accepted practices (as defined by research as well as what works in classrooms in this school) has changed, and it's making me a more effective teacher. I resented for a long time that Joan didn't use me more during this process, because I thought that I had a lot to offer. But I don't know how much my colleagues would have been able to learn from me because I was so resistant to learning anything from them. I'm pretty clear that this is my number-one issue to work on as a person and as a professional, but I'm determined to do better in the new *leadership position I have in the development of new core assessments and rubrics. [Rob consciously returns to the conversation with Henry, hoping that he has been as coherent in his discussion about understanding as he has been in his self-reflection.]*

Henry: Thanks for your insights and your time. I'm starting to get clearer on how you see the work that you've done and continue to do on core assessments and rubrics. Your explanation of understanding indicates that there's something going on in the classrooms here that is far richer than a test score alone can indicate.

Rob: I appreciate the compliment, but I respectfully disagree that assessment scores can't indicate that richness. In fact, that's my current hypothesis on why our core assessment scores have been lower than our state test results: our core assessments measure understanding which is more challenging and more meaningful than simply auditing discrete knowledge and skill.

With that, the conversation is over as Henry must move on to the scheduled meeting with Joan and the other teachers.

Susan, who is chairing the meeting, devotes the first 30 minutes of the agenda to reviewing key research that she has found on "closing the achievement gap"; she recommends readings for the committee members so they can all discuss how research and theory in the field should inform the staff's decisions regarding next steps in closing the gap. As the committee members begin to discuss the time line and how to share findings and progress with staff, Susan reflects to herself on how much has been accomplished this year and how much remains to be done. The staff is pulling together in ways that are exciting and rewarding for her, much more in alignment with what she expected when she first entered the profession seven years ago. The collective expertise of staff and the variety of well-founded perspectives are being harnessed in the work of moving toward the collective good. Not only are they all talking together, she thinks, but, more important, the conversations are focused, thoughtful, and rational. We are moving, she thinks, but we still have a long way to go before all the gaps are closed. She realizes that the journey to make the shared vision a reality will never end. As daunting as that thought is, she also finds the challenge of making this happen for every student exhilarating. She smiles as she reaffirms her commitment to the leadership role she has assumed in the school's transformation and to the changes in her own classroom that the innovation has required. She is brought back to the committee's discussion when someone, talking about scheduling difficulties, says, "The problems never seem to end. I just hope the next problem we have to deal with is different from the one we're solving now." She returns to the work at hand. The committee identifies tasks, divides them up, and sets up tentative dates for meetings over the summer.

Before adjourning the meeting, Susan asks Henry if he would like to say anything. Henry thanks them for sharing their time and their expertise. He tells them that he has learned a lot, and that the district continues to learn from all of the work being done by the school's staff. They should be proud. The teachers smile, and everyone heads off to different parts of the school or the parking lot. The official day has ended.

As Henry drives back to his office, he, too, finds himself reflecting. He is still a "new kid on the block" in the district but already feels pride as the head of the leadership team here. What a wonderful coincidence that he arrived as Joan's school was taking off. He is beginning to find real satisfaction from his conversations with Joan and is genuinely surprised by the sincerity and seriousness of her staff about assuming collective responsibility for the continuous improvement effort, and the higher student achievement they all see. Certainly the ideas of collective autonomy and collective accountability apply to the system as a whole. Certainly the concept of distributed leadership fits the district level too. But, he wonders, are we doing enough as a district to ensure that the gaps we are responsible for are being closed? Is it enough for me to be a critical friend by asking probing questions, or is there some formal staff development that needs to take place at the district and leadership levels? What do principals need to know, be able to do, and understand so that they can get their staff to raise academic achievement? What is my job in helping them to perform at higher levels? Have I relied too much on Ed to build these relationships for me? Am I anything more than the person they report to? Should I be? Can I be? Henry makes a mental note to talk with Ed tomorrow morning.

Summing Up and Looking Ahead

In the change process educators must keep the focus on improved student performance. Through this focus, collective accountability emerges. All staff, as a collective body, and all staff as individuals embrace accountability for achieving the desired results. As Schlechty (2001) advocates:

> Accountability for improvements in student learning should be long term and should reflect the principle of collective accountability. . . .More specifically [bullets added for emphasis]:
>   • Individual teachers can and should be held accountable for ensuring that what is taught is aligned with what is intended the students learn.
>   • Individual teachers also should be accountable for ensuring that the work they provide students improves continuously in terms of producing measurable student engagement, persistence, and satisfaction.
>   • Finally, school faculty as a group should be held accountable for the performance of students who have been in a school a sufficient amount of time for differences between [programs in] that school and other schools to make a difference. (p. 78)

Schools should measure their success in achieving the desired results by examining the evidence that students are more engaged and are achieving higher. "Clearly, students are our primary clients, given that the effectiveness of curriculum, assessment, and instructional designs is ultimately determined by their achievement of desired learnings" (Wiggins & McTighe, 1998, p. 7). Although our fictional school is just beginning its journey to achieve the desired results, it is clear that teachers and administrators have grown both individually and together in their capacity as systems thinkers, educators, leaders, and members of a larger school community.

Staff's next steps: The staff must begin the iterative process that is a trademark in any competent system. They must revisit data, revise the gaps to reflect the new reality, and refine (if necessary) the innovation to ensure they move again closer to their shared vision.

The reader's next step: With your school or your district in mind, consider the following questions:

➤ Is there accountability in your system? If so, does it focus on what your school community values?

➤ Who is accountable? Is it everyone, some staff, or no one? Is there an appropriate balance between collective accountability and individual accountability? How do you know?

➤ Is there accountability for both process and results? What's the evidence?

➤ Who leads the process? How widely is leadership shared? Is it shared widely enough?

➤ Is accountability data-driven? What data is used? Is it sufficient? If not, what additional data is needed?

Afterword

IT IS NOW TIME TO LEAVE OUR FICTIONAL SCHOOL TO RETURN TO THE REALITY of the systems that *do* exist. Every school or district must create its own success story, a story informed and illuminated by the six steps of continuous improvement. Each school must identify its core beliefs, develop a shared vision, measure the congruence between the current reality and the vision, determine the changes that will close any gaps, support teachers during the change process, and foster a culture of collective autonomy and accountability.

Establishing and maintaining a competent system may require fundamental shifts in the way your school community thinks about itself and defines the interrelationships among its members:

> ➤ From seeing parts of the system as discrete and independent to seeing them as part of a complex whole—*from unconnected thinking to systems thinking*
> ➤ From a reality based on unexamined assumptions (habits and traditions) to a reality based on both internal and external information (data, research, and theory)—*from perceived reality to information-based reality*
> ➤ From staff members focusing attention on their individual work in the school or classroom to sharing their work and critically examining practice with others as trusted members of the school community and always against the standards of excellence defined by the shared vision—*from isolation to collegiality*

➤ From acting on the basis of one's own interest or parochial vision to acting consistently in the interest of a shared vision—*from individual autonomy to collective autonomy*

➤ From seeing responsibility for student achievement only in terms of individual teacher effort to seeing student achievement as a product of a program and the school's effort around that program—*from individual autonomy to collective accountability*

To lead such complex and significant shifts, administrators and staff must carefully consider how to effectively use staff development time and resources to build capacity.

➤ Each staff development program or innovation must be seen as necessary learning before gaps between reality and vision can be closed.

➤ The action plan for completing the innovation must address all of the systemic issues raised by the change effort, and it must be treated as adaptable to new circumstances.

➤ As teachers experience the change, their concerns and their logistical needs must be honored and addressed.

➤ To be judged successful, staff development must result in staff members performing more competently individually and collectively, having a sense of professional pride in both kinds of performance, and ensuring that the shared vision comes closer to being realized.

Although following the six steps of continuous improvement is the cornerstone of developing a competent system, a competent system continues to thrive because of new challenges and the iterative process of continuous improvement.

> People make . . . fundamental transitions by having many opportunities to be exposed to ideas, to argue them to their own normative belief systems, to practice the behaviors that go with those values, to observe others practicing those behaviors, and, most importantly, to be successful at practicing in the presence of others (that is, to be seen to be successful). (Elmore, as cited in Fullan, 2001, pp. 130–131)

If administrators and staff become complacent about having achieved the transition from an incompetent system to a competent system, the system is vulnerable to falling back. The school must revisit core beliefs and shared visions for change and refinement, collect and examine new data and revisit old data, determine new staff development content to close gaps between reality and the shared vision, take teachers through the messy process of new learning, and build collective autonomy and accountability to meet even higher expectations for the school as a competent system. The beauty of continuous improvement is that it never stops, for envisioning the possibilities never ends.

APPENDIX

Operating Principles of the School as a Competent System

- ➤ For staff development to be effective, it must be an integral part of a deliberately developed continuous improvement effort.
- ➤ In a competent system, all staff members believe that what they have collectively agreed to do is challenging, possible, and worthy of the attempt.
- ➤ Each school is a complex living system with purpose.
- ➤ A competent system is driven by systems thinking.
- ➤ Every staff member must be regarded as a trusted colleague in the examination of assumptions and habitual practices.
- ➤ A shared vision articulates a coherent picture of what the school will look like when the core beliefs have been put into practice.
- ➤ The legitimacy of a shared vision is based on how well it represents all perspectives in the school community.
- ➤ Once staff members commit to the shared vision, they must gain clarity on their responsibility for achieving that vision.
- ➤ When staff members perceive data to be valid and reliable in collection and analysis, data both confirm what is working well and reveal the gaps between the current reality and the shared vision in a way that inspires collective action.
- ➤ All staff must see the content and process of staff development as a necessary means to achieve the desired end.
- ➤ It is not the number of innovations addressed in the staff development plan but rather the purposeful linkage among them that makes systemic change possible and manageable.
- ➤ Staff development must promote collective autonomy by embracing teaching as a distributed quality of the school.
- ➤ Planning must provide the clear, concrete direction necessary for systemic change while remaining flexible enough to accommodate the "nonrational" life in schools.
- ➤ Staff development must reflect the predictable stages of teacher concern about the complexities of moving from new learning to systemic consequences.
- ➤ A competent system proves itself when everyone within the system performs better as a result of the collective endeavors and accepts accountability for that improvement.

APPENDIX

B

Design Tool Used to Develop and Action Plan

Problem (gap between desired results and current performance)

Data we collected last year show that only 15 percent of teachers developed units that articulated alignment to relevant state content standards. Many teachers assume that alignment exists, but those assumptions are grounded more in a cursory read of the state standards or a belief that the units they designed are "what all good teachers should do" regardless of what the state department of education thinks. For students to do well on state assessments, however, teachers must mindfully integrate state standards into their unit and lesson designs. This is not only good practice but also is in alignment with our shared vision. Specifically:

- I will see evidence that students do well on tests of knowledge, measures of performance on open-ended prompts, and challenges requiring the use of knowledge and skill in new, important, and authentic ways.
- I will see a consistently high level of student achievement across this variety of assessment instruments.
- I will see (a) curriculum that sets high standards for all students, (b) instruction and teacher communication that foster the meeting of these standards, and (c) assessment that provides students the opportunity to demonstrate mastery.
- I will see curriculum that articulates key concepts, content, and skills that are necessary for all students to learn and instruction targeted to ensure all students learn these essentials.

Why this problem is a priority

This problem is an issue of both student achievement and equity. How can we expect students to do well on state assessments if teachers do not incorporate the standards for these into their planning and teaching? If we do not articulate the key concepts, content, and skills from state standards, we cannot ensure that all students are learning these essentials to be prepared for state assessments. We also need to be able to think about how the interrelationship among units ensures that the full range of state standards is addressed (instead of intensive focus on targeted areas).

How the innovations will help close the gap

Shared Vision

- I will see evidence that students do well at tests of knowledge, measures of performance on open-ended prompts, and challenges requiring the use of knowledge and skill in new, important, and authentic ways.
- I will see a consistently high level of student achievement across this variety of assessment instruments.
- I will see curriculum that sets high standards for all students, instruction and teacher communication that foster the meeting of these standards, and assessment that provides students the opportunity to demonstrate mastery.
- I will see curriculum that articulates key concepts, content, and skills that are necessary for all students to learn and instruction targeted to ensure all students learn these essentials.

Curriculum Mapping and Understanding by Design

- Curriculum map will be done for all grade levels and all subjects to ensure that all students are engaged in work that will prepare them to meet rigorous state and local expectations.
- Desired results for each unit include both state-determined knowledge and skill areas as well as local expectations for what students are expected to know, be able to do, and understand.
- Performance tasks and other evidence on curriculum map measure student performance on key knowledge, skills, and understandings as defined in the state content standards.
- State and local core assessments are listed on curriculum map to indicate when they are given in the scope and sequence and what they are designed to measure.
- Staff will be able to work with a broader range of state standards because they will be clearer on the standards incorporated in each of their units as well as by teachers at other grade levels.

Observable indicators that innovations have been successfully implemented

Through the lens of teacher instruction

- Instruction is driven by a need to "uncover" major concepts that provide the focus of the course, the program, and the discipline.
- The content knowledge and skills in the state or district standards are taught in a manner that encourages the development of the concept(s) or a conscious revisiting of the concept(s) so that the understanding of the concept(s) becomes more sophisticated.
- A variety of questioning strategies come to dominate, with the focus of the unit being established through the repeated use of "essential questions."

➤

Through the lens of student performance

- Students show through discussion and in their products a consistent struggle to make connections among the discrete knowledge and skills in a course.
- Students are discovering the conceptual framework of the discipline under study and the sense this framework gives to the knowledge and skills under study.
- Students see the concepts within this framework as important to their success in processing information and solving complex problems—in sum, addressing the challenges of a rich, productive life.

Planning for predictable staff concerns

There are too many state standards. How do I work them into my planning and teaching in more than a superficial way? (Informational Concern)

- Conduct a workshop on function of state standards in local curriculum that includes training on how to "unpack" content standards and how to bundle them around what you want students to "understand."
- Produce local document for each content area that reflects "unpacked" and bundled version of content standards linked to enduring understandings and essential questions.
- Meet in cross-grade-level teams to determine which grade levels will be responsible for which content standards. For those standards that will be incorporated on multiple grade levels, establish increased level of sophistication over time.

Planning and teaching to state standards compromises my ability to do the work that matters to me and to my students. The people who wrote those standards have no idea who we are—it is a sweeping generalization that works for no one. (Personal Concern)

- Devote time during faculty meetings and/or team time to compare state standards with collective and individual core beliefs and learning needs of students.
- Collectively discuss extent to which that comparison requires adjustment to curriculum scope and sequence.

How do I incorporate state standards into my unit plans and actual teaching? Is this the kind of thing I share with students? With parents? (Task Concern)

- Provide coaching to staff during development of curriculum maps as they work in teams to assign state standards to particular units.
- Conduct classroom visitations to see level of integration. Should see significant increase from last year's data (only 15% of staff could articulate which state standards were active in the design of instruction).
- Conduct full staff conversation about appropriate audience for content standards. Staff will decide on a policy together and accept responsibility for its implementation.

I want to prepare students for the state assessments but don't want to feel like I'm teaching to the test. How do I know that I'm doing my job and getting them ready? (Informational and Task Concerns)

- Conduct a workshop on the relationship between the state standards and the state assessments (contact state department of education for materials and/or possible speaker).
- Conduct a workshop on how to isolate key aspects of state assessments (vehicle for assessment, key knowledge and skill areas, etc.) and integrate them into local designs.
- Provide individual staff with key resources needed (individual and team planning time, coaching, etc.).

REFERENCES

Abbott, J. E. (1998). *Quality team learning for schools: A principal's perspective.* Milwaukee, WI: ASQ Quality Press.

Blase, J., & Kirby, P. C. (1992). *Bringing out the best in teachers: What effective principals do.* Newbury Park, CA: Corwin Press.

Bransford, J., Brown, A. L., & Cocking, R. R. (Eds.). (2000). *How people learn: Brain, mind, experience, and school.* Washington, DC: National Academy Press.

Brown, J. L., & Moffett, C. A. (1999). *The hero's journey: How educators can transform schools and improve learning.* Alexandria, VA: Association for Supervision and Curriculum Development.

Cook, W., Jr. (1986). *Certification program and strategic planning.* Arlington, VA: Cambridge Management Group, Inc. and AASA.

Covey, S. R. (1989). *The seven habits of highly effective people.* New York: Simon & Schuster.

Darling-Hammond, L. (1997). *The right to learn: A blueprint for creating schools that work.* San Francisco: Jossey-Bass.

DuFour, R. (2002). The learning-centered principal. *Educational Leadership, 59*(8), 12–15.

DuFour, R. & Eaker, R. (1998). *Professional learning communities at work: Best practices for enhancing student achievement.* Bloomington, IN: National Educational Service and ASCD.

Elmore, R. (Winter, 2000). *Building a new structure for school leadership.* Washington, DC: The Albert Shanker Institute.

Evans, R. (1996). *The human side of school change: Reform, resistance, and the real-life problems of innovation.* San Francisco: Jossey-Bass.

Fullan, M. (1993). *Change forces: Probing the depths of educational reform.* London: Falmer Press.

Fullan, M. (1999). *Change forces: The sequel.* London: Falmer Press.

Fullan, M. (2001). *Leading in a culture of change.* San Francisco: Jossey-Bass.

Fullan, M., & Stiegelbauer, S. (1991). *The new meaning of educational change.* New York: Teachers College Press.

Glickman, C. D. (1993). *Renewing America's schools.* San Francisco: Jossey-Bass.

Glickman, C. D. (2002). *Leadership for learning: How to help teachers succeed.* Alexandria, VA: Association for Supervision and Curriculum Development.

Hall, G. E., & Hord, S. M. (1987). *Change in schools: Facilitating the process.* Albany, NY: SUNY Press.

Hall, G. E., & Hord, S. M. (2001). *Implementing change: Patterns, principles, and potholes*. Boston: Allyn & Bacon.

Jacobs, H. H. (1997). *Mapping the big picture: Integrating curriculum and assessment K–12*. Alexandria, VA: Association for Supervision and Curriculum Development.

Joyce, B., & Showers, B. (2002). *Student achievement through staff development*. Alexandria, VA: Association for Supervision and Curriculum Development.

Lieberman, A., & Miller, L. (1999). *Teachers—transforming their world and their work*. New York: Teachers College Press.

Lightfoot, S. L. (1983). *The good high school: Portraits of character and culture*. New York: Basic Books, Inc.

Marzano, R. J. (2003). *What works in schools: Translating research into action*. Alexandria, VA: Association for Supervision and Curriculum Development.

McDonald, J. P. (1996). *Redesigning school: Lessons for the 21st century*. San Francisco: Jossey-Bass.

McTighe, J. (2003). *A summary of underlying theory and research base for Understanding by Design*. Unpublished manuscript.

McTighe, J., & Thomas, R. (2003). Backward design for forward action. *Educational Leadership (60)*5, 52–55.

National Staff Development Council. (2001). *Revised standards for staff development*. Oxford, OH: National Council for Staff Development.

Rossman, G. B., Corbett, H. D., & Firestone, W. A. (1988). *Change and effectiveness in schools: A cultural perspective*. Albany, NY: SUNY Press.

Sarason, S. B. (1990). *The predictable failure of educational reform: Can we change course before it's too late?* San Francisco: Jossey-Bass.

Sarason, S. B. (2002). *Educational reform: A self-scrutinizing memoir*. New York: Teachers College Press.

Schlechty, P. C. (2001). *Shaking up the school house: How to support and sustain educational innovation*. San Francisco: Jossey-Bass.

Schmoker, M. (1996). *Results: The key to continuous school improvement*. Alexandria, VA: Association for Supervision and Curriculum Development.

Schmoker, M. (2003, February 12). Planning for failure? Too much of schools' "improvement planning" misses the mark. *Education Week (22)*, 21.

Senge, P. (1990). *The fifth discipline: The art and practice of the learning organization*. New York: Doubleday.

Senge, P., Kleiner, A., Roberts, C., Ross, R. B., & Smith, B J. (1994). *The fifth discipline fieldbook: Strategies and tools for building a learning organization*. New York: Doubleday.

Senge, P., Cambron-McCabe, N., Lucas, T., Smith, B., Dutton, J., & Kleiner, A (2000). *Schools that learn: A fifth discipline fieldbook for educators, parents, and everyone who cares about education*. New York: Doubleday.

Sergiovanni, T. J. (1994). *Building community in schools*. San Francisco: Jossey-Bass.

Sergiovanni, T. J. (2000). *The lifeworld of leadership: Creating culture, community, and personal meaning in our schools*. San Francisco: Jossey-Bass.

Sparks, D. (2002). *Powerful professional development for teachers and principals*. National Staff Development Council.

Sparks, D., & Hirsh, S. (1997). *A new vision for staff development*. Alexandria, VA: Association for Supervision and Curriculum Development, and Oxford, OH: National Staff Development Council.

Spillane, J. P., Reiser, B. J., & Reimer, T. (2002). Policy implementation and cognition: Reframing and refocusing implementation research. *Review of Educational Research, 72*(3), 387–431.

Van den Berg, R. (2002). Teachers' meanings regarding educational practice. *Review of Educational Research, 72*(4), 577–625.

Wasley, P. A. (1991). *Teachers who lead: The rhetoric of reform and the realities of practice.* New York: Teachers College Press.

Wiggins, G. P., & McTighe, J. (1998). *Understanding by design.* Alexandria, VA: Association for Supervision and Curriculum Development.

Williams, B. (Ed.). (1996). *Closing the achievement gap: A vision for changing beliefs and practices.* Alexandria, VA: Association for Supervision and Curriculum Development.

Yero, J. L. (2002). *Teaching in mind: How teacher thinking shapes education.* Hamilton, MT: MindFlight Publishing.

Zmuda, A., & Tomaino, M. (2001). *The competent classroom: Aligning high school curriculum, standards and assessment—a creative teaching guide.* New York: Teachers College Press.

INDEX

Information contained in figures is indicated by an italic *f* following the page number.

ABOUT THE AUTHORS

Allison Zmuda is an education consultant for ASCD in Alexandria, Virginia, and Director, Division of Teaching and Learning for the Capitol Region Education Council in Hartford, Connecticut, where she works with staff to design curriculum that is in alignment with state content standards and serves the system's mission. She began her work in education as a high school social studies teacher in Sandy Hook, Connecticut. Inspired by her work in the classroom and on curriculum development, Zmuda coauthored *The Competent Classroom* (2001), jointly published by Teachers College Press and the National Education Association; and *High Stakes High School: A Guide for the Perplexed Parent* (2001), published by Simon and Schuster. She also coauthored "A Contract for the High School Classroom," which appeared in the March 1999 issue of *Educational Leadership* and was reprinted in the *Educational Leadership Best of 1999* issue. Zmuda lives in Woodbury, Connecticut, where she continues to read, write, and think aloud with educators whom she is honored to also call friends. She may be contacted by phone at (203) 263-7968 or by e-mail at azmuda@crec.org.

Robert Kuklis is a retired public school administrator who currently teaches a graduate course on curriculum at Sacred Heart University in Fairfield, Connecticut. He also supervises administrative interns at Pace University in White Plains, New York, and student teachers at Teachers College, Columbia University, in New York City. He served as a public school teacher for 18 years, the last 9 as a social studies department chairperson. During his years as a teacher, he piloted units and wrote a unit for the Committee on the Study of History, a group promoting inquiry in the classroom. Kuklis was a high school administrator for 13 years and finished his public school administrative career by serving as an assistant superintendent for curriculum and instruction in Newtown, Connecticut, for six and one-half years. While a principal in the 1980s, he worked as a lead facilitator for the Principals Academy, Syracuse University/New York State Consortium for School Improvement; and in the 1990s, he served as a principal of a high school being researched by the Coalition of Essential Schools, the research resulting in the book *Kids and School Reform*. As assistant superintendent in Newtown, Kuklis provided the leadership for developing and implementing standards-based curriculum throughout the district. Kuklis currently resides in New Rochelle, New York, and can be reached by phone at (914) 235-4840 or by e-mail at bobkuklis@ optonline.net.

Everett Kline is a member of the ASCD faculty of consultants. Before joining ASCD he worked as a senior staff associate for the Center for Learning, Assessment and School Structure. He began his work in education as a history teacher in the school district of South Orange and Maplewood, New Jersey. During this time, Princeton University honored Kline as a master teacher. In the South Orange/Maplewood district he also served as chair of the high school social studies department and Director of Secondary Education. When he left that district to consult, he was Assistant Superintendent for Instruction and Learning. His work on change in that district was chronicled in an article he was asked to write for *Primary Voices*, a journal of the National Council of Teachers of English. Kline lives in Princeton, New Jersey. As director of his own consulting firm, Understanding[4], he remains active in the field, thriving on the intellectual challenge of working with teachers, administrators, and educational theorists throughout the United States and around the world. He can be contacted at (609) 279-1321 or by e-mail at Everett@understanding4.com.

Related ASCD Resources: Transforming Schools

At the time of publication, the following ASCD resources were available; for the most up-to-date information about ASCD resources, go to http://www.ascd.org. ASCD stock numbers are noted in parentheses.

Multimedia
Promoting Learning Through Student Data study group kit developed by Marian Leibowitz (#999004)

Networks
Visit the ASCD Web site (http://www.ascd.org) and search for "networks" for information about professional educators who have formed groups around topics like "Restructuring Schools" and "Systems Thinking & Chaos Theory." Look in the "Network Directory" for current facilitators' addresses and phone numbers.

Print Products
Closing the Achievement Gap: A Vision for Changing Beliefs and Practices edited by Belinda Williams (#102101)
Dimensions of Learning Teacher's Manual, 2nd Edition, by Robert J. Marzano and Debra J. Pickering (#197133)
Motivating Teachers and Students in an Era of Standards by Richard Sagor (#103009)
Understanding by Design by Grant Wiggins and Jay McTighe (#198199)
The Understanding by Design Handbook by Jay McTighe and Grant Wiggins (#199030)
What Works In Schools: Translating Research into Action by Robert J. Marzano (#102271)

Videotapes
What Works in Schools series by Robert J. Marzano (#403047)

For more information, visit us on the World Wide Web (http://www.ascd.org), send an e-mail message to member@ascd.org, call the ASCD Service Center (1(800) 933-ASCD or 703-578-9600, then press 2), send a fax to (703) 575-5400, or write to Information Services, ASCD, 1703 N. Beauregard St., Alexandria, VA 22311-1714 USA.